Co-Parentir

Narcissist:

A Life-Changing Guide to Protect Your Child, Set Strong Boundaries, and Keep Your Sanity after Divorcing a Narcissistic Ex

Melanie Wolfkill

Table of Contents

Introduction

"I constantly feel like I'm walking on eggshells."

"My ex manipulates every situation and drives me crazy."

"I'm worried every day about my child's well-being."

"Why can't they see the harm they're causing?"

"I feel exhausted and drained."

"My boundaries are never respected."

"How can I protect my child from their toxic influence?"

"I dread every new argument and confrontation."

"I feel overwhelmed and lost, not knowing how to move forward."

Do these phrases sound familiar to you?

If you're reading these lines, you know what it means to prioritize the wellbeing of your children while trying to keep your own mental health intact. Co-parenting with a narcissist involves facing continuous emotional manipulation: moments of apparent calm followed by bursts of anger, subtle manipulations, and power plays that leave deep scars. Every discussion can turn into a battlefield, where the real goal is not to solve the problem, but to maintain control.

Your child observes all this, absorbing the tension and conflict like a sponge. You begin to notice changes in their behavior: insomnia, anxiety, difficulties at school. Each sign breaks your heart and makes you feel powerless. You try to compensate with love and attention, but the emotional burden you carry is enormous. You feel trapped in an endless cycle of stress and worry, with very little support or understanding from others.

Your friendships have cooled because no one seems to truly understand what you're going through. Every day feels like a solitary struggle to maintain a semblance of normality. Your mental health is continuously at risk from your ex-partner, and you start to doubt yourself and your abilities as a parent. Every decision is laden with anxiety, every interaction with your ex leaves you exhausted and defeated.

If you do not address this situation, your well-being and that of your child will suffer irreparably. But how can you protect your child and yourself from this toxic cycle? This book will provide the answers you are looking for.

Imagine a different reality. Imagine being able to establish clear and healthy boundaries with your narcissistic ex, boundaries that not only protect you but also your child. Each interaction, instead of being an exhausting battle, becomes a manageable conversation. You have the tools to stay calm and assertive, avoiding emotional pitfalls and manipulations. Each time you put these new skills into practice, you feel a growing confidence in yourself and in your role as a parent.

Your child begins to thrive in this more stable and secure environment. You notice that they sleep better, are more peaceful, and focused at school. Their anxiety decreases, and they start to smile and play as they should. You see their well-being improving day by day, and this gives you new strength and determination. You know you are doing everything possible to protect them and ensure a calm and happy life.

Imagine your personal life improving. Your friendships strengthen. Imagine feeling more relaxed and at peace with yourself, capable of facing daily challenges with serenity. Imagine regaining your mental health and beginning to live a more balanced and fulfilling life.

The results are astonishing: not only do you regain your inner peace, but your child also thrives. Sleepless nights and constant conflicts become a distant memory. Your days are filled with moments of serenity and shared joy. You see your child growing up in a loving and secure environment, and this alone makes every effort and sacrifice worthwhile. This transformation is not an unattainable dream. It's a possible reality that this book will guide you to achieve. Through practical strategies and advice based on experience, you'll discover how to move from living in a state of constant alertness to a life of serenity and control.

I am Melanie Wolfkill, and my personal and professional experience has led me to write this book. I have personally lived through the emotional devastation of a marriage with a narcissist and the nightmare of co-parenting with one. My mission is to help parents like you find the strength and resources to protect their children and themselves.

During my journey, I worked as a family counselor, specializing in narcissistic dynamics and managing conflictual relationships. I have seen how much pain and confusion a narcissistic ex-spouse can cause, not only to the partner but especially to the children involved. The stories I've listened to and the people I've helped have taught me a lot about how to successfully handle these situations.

I decided to write this book because I know how difficult it is to face these battles alone. When I found myself in that position, I wished I had a guide, someone to show me that there was a way out and that it was possible to build a peaceful and stable life for myself and my child. This book is the result of years of study, experience, and the desire to share what I have learned with you.

I am not just a professional, but a person who has walked the same path you are on now. My hope is that through the pages of this book, you can find the guidance and support you need to overcome these challenges and build a better future for you and your child.

This book is not a magic solution. You won't find quick or easy answers without putting in the effort. Co-parenting with a narcissist is complex and requires time, patience, and a lot of introspection. You won't find abstract theories or generic advice here. Every suggestion and strategy is based on real experiences and what actually works. I will provide concrete examples and practical techniques that you can implement immediately.

This book does not focus on self-pity or blaming the past. Our focus will be on the present and the future. I will show you how to build a safe and positive environment for you and your child, regardless of your ex's behavior. I won't promise that it will be easy, but I assure you that it will be worth it. Every step forward you take, every boundary you establish, every moment of peace you create for your child will be a victory. And these victories are possible, with the right guidance and support.

Lastly, this book is not about your ex. It is about you and your child. It is a guide to reclaiming control of your life and creating a brighter future, regardless of the difficulties your ex may try to impose. It is a journey towards healing and strength, and you have already taken the first step by reading these words.

If you see yourself in these pages, if you feel the weight of your situation and long for a change, this book is written for you. Don't let another day pass under the shadow of co-parenting with a narcissist. It's time to discover the strategies that will guide you toward a life of serenity and control. Take the book in hand, immerse yourself in its pages, and begin your journey toward a better reality. Not only is it possible, but with the right support and the correct information, it is within reach. For you and your child, the time to act is now. Discover how to transform your life. Start today.

Chapter 1:
Understanding Narcissistic Abuse

Have you ever felt that someone in your life makes you feel inadequate, constantly criticized, or manipulated? It could be a colleague, a friend, a partner, or even a family member. That overwhelming feeling of never being enough might be a sign of narcissistic behavior. Understanding narcissism and narcissistic abuse is essential to recognize and address these toxic dynamics.

Narcissism is not just vanity or self-centeredness, but a set of behaviors that can have a devastating impact on those around. Narcissists are characterized by a profound lack of empathy, a sense of superiority, and an incessant need for admiration. These individuals tend to view others as tools to satisfy their own needs, ignoring the feelings and needs of others.

Consider, for example, Laura's story. She thought she had the perfect relationship with Mark. At first, he was charming and attentive, but over time, Laura began to feel increasingly isolated and devalued. Mark constantly criticized her decisions, her friendships, and even her appearance. Every attempt to discuss her feelings was met with arrogance or manipulated to make her feel guilty. Laura didn't understand what was happening until she discovered the term "narcissistic abuse."

Narcissistic abuse is a complex and often underestimated phenomenon. It manifests through a series of behaviors that cause profound psychological harm to the victims. These behaviors include devaluation, emotional manipulation, isolation, and cold indifference. Victims of narcissistic abuse can feel confused, insecure, and deeply depressed, often developing symptoms similar to post-traumatic stress disorder.

One of the biggest challenges in recognizing narcissistic abuse is that narcissists are often skilled manipulators. They can present themselves as charming and confident, earning the trust and admiration of others. However, behind this facade lies a cold and calculating personality, ready to exploit anyone for their own advantage.

To distinguish between narcissism and narcissistic personality disorder, it's helpful to understand that the disorder is characterized by a set of behaviors that cause significant distress or impairment in the person's daily life. However, many narcissists do not experience obvious distress or impairment. In fact, they often achieve success and enjoy social admiration, masking their pathology. This makes it particularly difficult to diagnose narcissistic personality disorder, as these individuals do not recognize they have a problem and attribute difficulties in their relationships to others.

The importance of understanding narcissism and narcissistic abuse lies in the ability to recognize these behaviors and protect oneself. People who are victims of narcissistic abuse face a difficult path of awareness and healing, but the first step is always recognizing the problem. Only then can they begin to build a healthier life, free from manipulation and abuse.

Realizing that narcissism is a widespread and real problem is the first step to protecting oneself and helping those who are victims. Through education and awareness, we can start recognizing the signs of narcissism and narcissistic abuse in our daily lives, paving the way for healthier and more fulfilling relationships.

The 4 Stages of Narcissistic Abuse

Imagine meeting someone who seems like the perfect partner: attentive, affectionate, and totally devoted to you. At first, everything seems like a dream. Then, slowly, the dream turns into a nightmare. If you find yourself wondering how you ended up in such a situation, you're not alone. This is a common story for those in relationships with narcissists. Understanding the stages of narcissistic abuse is crucial for recognizing it and breaking free from its destructive cycle.

Idealization Phase

During the idealization phase, the narcissist wins over the victim through charming and seductive behavior. This stage is characterized by excessive attention, constant compliments, and romantic gestures. The narcissist is extremely affectionate and seems to know exactly your desires and needs. It's easy to fall into this trap, feeling flattered and appreciated like never before. The victim, caught up in this whirlwind of positive emotions, lowers their defenses and becomes completely dependent on the narcissist.

During this period, the narcissist adopts a mask of perfection, behaving in a way that satisfies every emotional need of the victim. They organize romantic evenings, give unexpected attention, and demonstrate a seemingly profound understanding of the other's emotions. This creates an intense bond and emotional dependency, making it difficult to see the warning signs. The idealization phase is designed to create a rapid and intense connection, making the victim feel incredibly special and loved.

Devaluation Phase

The devaluation phase begins when the narcissist feels they have total control. The affectionate and flattering behaviors give way to criticism and devaluation. Every little mistake is magnified and used to undermine your self-esteem. In this phase, the narcissist employs techniques like gaslighting to make you doubt yourself and your perception of reality. Accusations, manipulations, and mind games start, making you feel constantly inadequate. The victim, confused and insecure, desperately tries to regain the narcissist's approval and affection, often without success.

In this stage, the narcissist stops pretending to be perfect and begins to reveal their true self. Criticism becomes more frequent and targeted to undermine the victim's confidence. Demeaning comments about physical appearance, intelligence, work abilities, and social relationships are common. The narcissist might also begin isolating the victim from friends and family, making them even more dependent on the toxic relationship. Devaluation is not just verbal but can also manifest through passive-aggressive behaviors, like silent treatment or blatant indifference.

Discard Phase

When the narcissist decides you're no longer useful or they've found a new source of narcissistic supply, the discard phase begins. This phase can be particularly cruel and sudden. The narcissist abandons you without any warning, leaving you in a state of shock and despair. They might disappear from your life without explanation or attempt to destroy your reputation with false and defamatory accusations. The victim, already weakened by devaluation, must face a brutal and unexpected abandonment.

The discard can be insidiously planned. The narcissist might gradually decrease contact and affection, psychologically preparing you for abandonment, or they might vanish from your life overnight, leaving you with many questions and no answers. In some cases, the narcissist might start a smear campaign against you, involving mutual friends, family, and colleagues to further isolate you and protect their own image. This behavior aims to destroy your self-esteem and ensure you lack the support needed to recover.

Repetition Cycle

Often, the narcissist might try to re-engage after the discard phase in what is known as "hoovering." Promises of change and temporarily affectionate behaviors are used to suck you back into the cycle of abuse. If you give in, the cycle of idealization, devaluation, and discard will repeat, often with even more devastating consequences. It is a cycle that can seem endless and difficult to break.

During "hoovering," the narcissist might use various tactics to convince you to return, such as affectionate letters, gifts, apparent apologies, and declarations of eternal love. These gestures are designed to make you feel the narcissist has changed and that this time will be different. However, once you are back in the relationship, the cycle resumes, and the promises made during "hoovering" are quickly forgotten. The narcissist's ability to alternate between phases of intense love and cruelty creates an emotional dependency in the victim, who clings to the rare positive phases, hoping for lasting change.

Recognizing and understanding the stages of narcissistic abuse is one of the crucial steps towards healing. With the right support, it is possible to break the cycle of abuse and build a healthier, happier life, free from the narcissist's manipulations. You are not alone in this journey, and with determination and help, you can regain control of your life.

The Consequences of Narcissistic Abuse

The consequences of narcissistic abuse can be devastating and long-lasting. Victims often experience a range of psychological and behavioral effects that deeply impact their daily lives. Understanding these effects is essential to recognize the severity of the abuse and seek the necessary support for healing.

One of the first consequences of such abuse is the erosion of self-esteem. Through constant devaluation and criticism, the narcissist makes the victim feel inadequate and unworthy of love or respect. This leads to profound insecurity and a sense of inferiority that can persist long after the abusive relationship has ended. The victim may start to doubt their abilities and self-worth, developing a paralyzing self-criticism.

Another characteristic of this abuse is mental confusion. Victims often feel like they are "going crazy" due to the constant manipulation and distortion of reality by the narcissist. This state of confusion can lead to a loss of trust in their own judgment and perceptions, making it difficult to make autonomous decisions and trust others.

Anxiety is another common effect. Victims live in a constant state of alert, worried about the narcissist's unpredictable reactions. This anxiety can manifest as sleep difficulties, concentration problems, and a general sense of apprehension. The fear of provoking the narcissist's anger or disappointment becomes an obsession, making it difficult to relax or enjoy moments of peace.

Depression is a frequent consequence. Constant invalidation and a sense of helplessness can lead to deep feelings of sadness and despair. The victim may feel trapped in a situation with no way out, experiencing a loss of interest in activities they once enjoyed. This depressive state can negatively affect their ability to function in daily life, compromising work, social relationships, and self-care.

Victims often develop symptoms of post-traumatic stress as well. These symptoms can include flashbacks, nightmares, hypervigilance, and an exaggerated response to stimuli that remind them of the abuse. The victim may feel constantly threatened, even in safe situations, and find it hard to trust people. This post-traumatic stress can last for years and require specific therapeutic intervention to manage effectively.

Another significant effect is social isolation. Narcissists often try to isolate their victims from their friends and family, reducing their support system. This isolation increases the narcissist's power over the victim, making them more dependent and vulnerable. The victim may feel alone and without resources, making it even harder to seek help or leave the abusive relationship.

Subsequent relationships can also be negatively influenced by the experience of narcissistic abuse. The fear of being manipulated or devalued again can lead the victim to avoid new relationships or choose partners who repeat similar dynamics. It is important for victims to work on their self-esteem and trust through therapy and the support of friends and family to break this cycle.

Narcissistic abuse can also have physical impacts. The chronic stress associated with this type of abuse can manifest in physical symptoms such as headaches, gastrointestinal problems, muscle tension, and fatigue. The victim may neglect their physical health due to depression or anxiety, further exacerbating health issues.

The victim of narcissistic abuse experiences a combination of emotional, psychological, and physical problems that can persist for a long time. Recognizing these effects is the first step towards healing.

The 5 Stages of Grief in Divorcing a Narcissist

Going through a divorce is one of the most challenging times in a person's life, often compared to events like the death of a loved one. However, when it comes to divorcing a narcissist, the situation becomes even more complex and painful. It is crucial to understand the five emotional stages you go through during this process to recognize the signs and deal with them as effectively as possible.

Denial, anger, bargaining, depression, and acceptance are the five main stages everyone goes through during a divorce. These stages, known as Elizabeth Kubler-Ross's model, are particularly relevant when dealing with a narcissist. The initial denial can stem from the fear of facing reality and the consequences of the divorce, while anger can be fueled by perceived injustice and the harm caused by the narcissist. Bargaining represents the attempt to find a way out or reconcile the situation, often manipulated by the narcissist. Depression arises when confronting the reality of the marriage's failure, and acceptance is the final stage, where inner peace is reached and one looks forward to a new life.

Understanding these stages not only helps recognize and manage one's emotions but also aids in making more informed decisions during the divorce. During this period of great emotional turmoil, it is essential to be clear and rational in choices, despite the difficulties. Being prepared and aware of one's feelings can make a significant difference in the healing process and in building a new life after the divorce.

Stage 1: Denial - "This is not happening"

The first stage of divorcing a narcissist is denial. Initially, there is a strong fear of what might happen. This fear is fueled by the awareness that once the divorce process starts, the narcissist will turn against us, making us their number one enemy. There is the fear that they might expose us, try to turn the world against us, creating emotional, physical, and spiritual hell.

During this phase, there is often denial about the reality of the situation. One tries to minimize the problems, thinking that maybe they are not so bad or that one can live with them. There is hope that the narcissist might change, that things might get better. This denial is a defense mechanism that helps avoid facing the painful truth of the deteriorating relationship.

Thoughts like, "Maybe it's not that bad," or "I can live with this," or "This person can change," are common. There is a tendency to deny that the relationship is really as problematic as it seems. This stage of denial can last a long time, preventing one from taking the necessary steps to protect oneself and begin the healing process.

Recognizing denial is the first step to overcoming it. It is essential to face reality, no matter how painful it might be, and prepare to tackle the challenges that lie ahead. Only by accepting the truth can one start the journey towards a new life, free from the toxic influence of the narcissist.

Stage 2: Anger - "Why this is happening "

The second stage of divorcing a narcissist is anger. In this phase, you start to question why your partner has to be so terrible and why they can't change. You feel frustrated about everything the narcissist has ruined: the infidelity, the wasted time, and the negative impact on your children. The anger is fueled by feeling deprived of a significant part of your life and by resentment towards the narcissist for not doing more, like earning more money or not wasting it.

Many people stay stuck in this phase for a long time, unable to let go of the sense of injustice. There is a mistaken belief that forgiving or moving past the anger would let the narcissist "get away" with their actions. However, it is crucial to understand that overcoming anger is primarily about your own emotional health and well-being.

Anger can be paralyzing, but it is necessary to confront it to free yourself from the poison and toxicity it brings. It's important to distinguish between the desire for what is right under the law and the need not to let fear and emotion influence your decisions. Justice should not be confused with prolonged resentment or vengeance.

Overcoming anger is essential to move on to the next stages of divorce. You need to find a balance between the desire for fairness and the need for inner peace, allowing the law to take its course without being overwhelmed by negative emotions.

Stage 3: Bargaining - "Wtf is happening?"

The third stage of divorcing a narcissist is bargaining. In this phase, you can enter dangerous territory because the narcissist might start to be nice again, trying to "hoover" the relationship, which means re-attracting their victim. This can make you weak, leading you to think that maybe things could work out, that maybe it won't be so bad, or that you might be able to maintain an amicable relationship.

Often, you fall into the trap of believing that if you give in on certain points, the narcissist will recognize your value and reciprocate. However, this is a dangerous illusion. When negotiating with a narcissist, giving too much at the beginning will never lead to getting anything in return. The narcissist will take everything they can without acknowledging your value or giving anything back.

During this bargaining phase, you might also experience a return to the "honeymoon" phase, which is often followed by rejection. This can make you feel even worse, as if you have been rejected again. Bargaining can make you feel even more lonely and sad, amplifying the sense of rejection.

It is crucial to recognize that this bargaining phase will not lead to a lasting or positive solution. Instead, it is important to stand your ground and not give in to the narcissist's manipulations. Only by doing so can you move towards healing and a healthier, more peaceful life, away from the toxic dynamics of a relationship with a narcissist.

Stage 4: Depression - "Why this happened"

The fourth stage of divorcing a narcissist is depression. This is one of the most challenging phases because it represents the emotional low point. After going through denial, anger, and bargaining, you are faced with the reality of the end of the marriage. During this phase, you feel lonely, sad, and often blame yourself.

You question whether you have wasted your life, whether your partner ever truly loved you, or if you gave up too much during the divorce. You wonder if you made poor choices, like hiring a worse lawyer than your ex or spending too much on the divorce. You are overwhelmed with remorse and regret, reliving every moment, every decision made, every mistake.

In this stage, it's common to dwell on the "what ifs" and "buts," thinking about how things could have gone differently. It's easy to fall into a spiral of negative thoughts, constantly replaying what went wrong and what you could have done differently. However, it's important not to get too caught up in these thoughts, as they cannot change the past.

Instead, it's essential to focus on building a new life and creating new memories, starting to shape a different and more peaceful future. This also means avoiding hearing stories about what your ex is doing with their new life, as this will only increase your sense of sadness and loneliness.

Stage 5: Acceptance - "Oh no its that asshole again"

The fifth stage of divorcing a narcissist is acceptance. This stage represents reaching inner peace and being able to look forward to a new life. You know you have reached this stage when you can see your ex-partner without feeling any intense emotions, neither positive nor negative. You simply feel indifferent, as if they were just another person.

Reaching acceptance means you have finally managed to build a new, independent, and fulfilling life. At this point, your ex-partner has their life, and you have yours, and this no longer disturbs you. You have created a space for yourself where you feel complete and satisfied without needing the narcissist around.

This stage is not only a sign that you have overcome the divorce but also that you have rediscovered yourself. You have gone through denial, anger, bargaining, and depression, and now you are ready to live a new life, free from the toxic dynamics that characterized your relationship with the narcissist.

Acceptance allows you to look to the future with hope and engage in new activities and relationships that bring joy and satisfaction. It is the moment when you realize that you have become the person you were meant to be, free from the negative influence of the narcissist.

Reaching acceptance is a long and difficult process, but once you achieve it, you can finally say that you have completely overcome the divorce and are ready for a new life full of opportunities.

Recognizing the Signs of a Narcissistic Co-Parent

Recognizing the signs of narcissistic abuse is crucial for protecting yourself and breaking the cycle of manipulation and devaluation. Narcissists can be difficult to identify because they often present a charming and confident image, earning the trust and admiration of others. However, there are distinct traits that can help recognize narcissistic behavior.

A typical narcissist has several well-defined characteristics. First and foremost, they exhibit a lack of empathy. This person cannot understand or share the feelings of others, treating others' emotions with indifference or disdain. A narcissist is often grandiose, with an exaggerated sense of their own importance and abilities. This individual is also arrogant and believes they deserve special treatment.

Another key characteristic of a narcissist is the constant need for admiration and validation. They continually seek approval from others, and when they don't receive it, they may react with anger or frustration. Narcissists are often superficial, focused on appearances and material possessions rather than deep, meaningful relationships.

There are two main types of narcissism: grandiose narcissism and vulnerable narcissism. Grandiose narcissism is the more easily recognizable type: the narcissist is flashy, confident, and eager to attract attention. On the other hand, vulnerable narcissism is subtler and less apparent. This type of narcissist is often resentful, sullen, and sees themselves as a victim of life. They feel entitled to more and perceive the world as unjust. Both forms of narcissism share a lack of empathy and a sense of superiority but manifest in different ways.

An important distinction to make is between someone with narcissistic traits and someone with narcissistic personality disorder (NPD). NPD is a clinical condition where narcissistic behaviors cause significant distress or impairment in the person's daily life. However, many people with narcissistic traits do not experience these problems. In fact, they often achieve success and enjoy social admiration, thus masking their pathology. This difference is crucial because a diagnosis of NPD requires that the narcissistic behavior causes obvious problems in the person's life.

Recognizing the signs of narcissistic abuse in a relationship can be difficult, but there are some key indicators to watch for. The narcissist tends to belittle and devalue the other person, reducing their self-esteem. They use emotional manipulation to control and dominate their partner, making the other person feel guilty or inadequate. They often isolate their partner from friends and family, increasing their power and control over the victim.

In a co-parenting context, recognizing the signs of a narcissistic co-parent is crucial for protecting both yourself and your children. Specific behaviors of narcissistic co parents include:

- Demanding to know all plans and activities that occur during the other parent's time.

- Refusing to hand the children over for the other parent's time.

- Texting or calling the other parent or the children nonstop during the other parent's time.

- Questioning the children about everything that happened with the other parent, including what they ate, where they went, who they saw, and then starting fights with the other parent.

- Telling the children to record or take photos of the other parent, the house, activities, etc., and sending them to the narcissistic parent to file unfounded claims with child protective services.

- Involving the children in mental and psychological games, such as planning elaborate vacations or being the parent with no rules or punishments, and comparing everything to the other parent's ability to plan or provide.

- Harassing or cyberbullying the other parent's friends, family, or new romantic partner.

- Attempting to isolate the children from seeing anyone the narcissistic parent doesn't "approve" of, even without reason. This could also include other family members or the other parent's friends.

- Insisting on celebrating holidays or special events together "as a family" despite the other parent not agreeing. Even when told no, the narcissistic parent will either show up ("It's a public event!") or guilt the children and the other parent.

- Alternately, trying to control who shows up to events. ("You can come, but your new wife isn't allowed.")

- Telling the children their other parent "won't allow them" to be a family or spend time together, portraying themselves as the suffering victim.

- Refusing to abide by the custody schedule or rules, such as moving school districts or failing to give notice about taking the child out of state.

- Changing their schedules or the children's schedules without consulting the other parent and informing them of changes at the last minute, forcing the other parent to accommodate and change their schedule.

- Harassing and cyberbullying the other parent until they give in to demands.

- Threatening to bankrupt or ruin the other parent.

- Attempting to seduce the other parent when a new relationship is started.

- Manipulating text conversations and presenting out-of-context statements to people to ruin the other parent's reputation, friendships, or relationships.

- Spreading lies and rumors about the other parent or the other parent's new romantic partner to make themselves look better, sometimes using this to cause problems at work or in court. Narcissistic exes and co-parents have been known to accuse the other parent of drug and alcohol addiction, domestic abuse, rape, and stalking. These unfounded claims do nothing but complicate an already stressful and messy situation, irreparably damaging reputations.

Understanding and recognizing these signs is the first step to protecting yourself and your children from a narcissistic co-parent. This awareness is fundamental for taking concrete actions and improving the emotional and psychological well-being of everyone involved.

Why Do Narcissists Get Married ?

One of the main reasons narcissists get married is the importance of social image. We live in a society where marriage is a recognized social norm, and narcissists are deeply aware of these social expectations. Nothing is more important to a narcissist than the image they project to others, and they will go to great lengths to build and maintain a perfect image. Marrying the "right" person is a fundamental part of this strategy. They seek partners who contribute to the image they want to create, partners who can be displayed as trophies, reflections of their supposed perfection.

But social image is not the only reason. For a narcissist, marriage also represents a way to have absolute control over their partner. Initially, the partner is unaware of the narcissist's true intentions. The narcissist views marriage as a means to possess an inexhaustible source of narcissistic supply. The partner becomes a resource from which they can continuously draw, without limits. From this perspective, marriage is seen as a contract that guarantees the continuous availability of the partner to meet the narcissist's needs.

Control is also manifested through manipulation and coercion. Narcissists carefully select their partners, seeking individuals who can be manipulated and transformed into ideal versions of submissive spouses. They never truly consider the partner's needs; they are solely focused on their own needs. The partner is seen as an object, a tool to satisfy the narcissist's demands, as they skillfully manipulate reality to maintain control.

Another reason narcissists get married is the security of the marital bond. They view marriage as a chain that binds the partner to them indissolubly. They firmly believe that the marriage contract will ensure the partner will never leave them, thus guaranteeing they will never be alone or abandoned. For them, this contract represents tangible proof that they will always have someone by their side, regardless of how they behave.

Marriage, therefore, becomes a gilded prison for the partner, who often finds themselves trapped in a relationship based on manipulation and control. The narcissist uses this relationship to build and maintain an impeccable public image, while behind closed doors, the partner suffers in silence, often unaware of the extent of the psychological manipulation they are subjected to.

Narcissists do not get married for love, but for power and control. They use marriage as a tool to maintain a perfect social image and ensure a constant source of narcissistic supply. Their need for control and fear of abandonment drive them to create bonds that, for the partner, often become a painful and difficult trap to escape.

Why Do Narcissists Have Kids ?

The primary reason narcissists decide to have children is surprisingly simple and deeply unsettling: they seek a source of emotional supply. For narcissists, children represent an endless reservoir of personal gratification and a means to enhance their social image. There is no genuine desire to care for and raise an autonomous individual; rather, there is a desire to have someone who can reflect their "grandiosity" and fulfill their selfish needs.

Narcissists view children as trophies, as extensions of themselves that they can showcase to gain praise and recognition. Every success of the child becomes an opportunity for the narcissistic parent to boast and feel superior. "Look at what I've created" is a common thought in the narcissist's mind, deriving an unhealthy sense of omnipotence from their children's achievements. This is what makes narcissistic behavior so nauseating and revealing at the same time: they do not see children as individuals with their own rights and needs but as property to manipulate and use.

Another motivation driving narcissists to become parents is the desire to create chaos and divisions within the family. Children can be used as pawns in emotional power games, where the narcissist creates conflicts and rivalries among siblings, or between the partner and the children themselves. This chaos serves to maintain control and ensure that the attention always remains focused on them. Every little dispute, every internal competition within the family, feeds the narcissist's need to feel at the center of the universe.

Additionally, narcissists may see children as an opportunity to reinforce their manipulations over their partner. Having children with a narcissist often means becoming a "single parent" within a couple, as the narcissistic parent systematically avoids responsibilities and leaves the burden of parenting to the other partner. This forced isolation strengthens the emotional and practical dependence of the non-narcissistic partner, further trapping them in the abusive relationship.

Narcissists also find emotional supply in their children through inducing guilt and exerting control. Love and attention are given conditionally, based on the child's performance and obedience. This creates a perverse cycle where the child is constantly seeking the parent's approval but never receives it in a stable and secure way. The result is profound emotional trauma that can persist throughout life, making it difficult for the child to establish healthy and trusting relationships in the future.

Finally, the presence of children allows narcissists to maintain a social facade of normalcy and respectability. Being a parent gives them a perfect cover to mask their true pathological self behind the image of a devoted and loving parent. This carefully constructed and maintained image can deceive many, including friends, family, and colleagues, who only see what the narcissist wants to show. The reality of their actions and emotional abuse remains hidden behind a curtain of apparent normalcy.

Narcissists decide to have children not out of love or a desire to create a family, but to fulfill their selfish needs for gratification, control, and manipulation. Children become tools to feed their sense of grandiosity and to maintain control within the family, causing deep and lasting emotional damage.

Can Narcissists Be Good Parents?

Effective parenting requires a combination of patience, understanding, consideration, compassion, and calmness. These attributes are essential for ensuring a child grows up in a healthy and loving environment. However, when it comes to narcissistic parents, these fundamental elements are completely absent.

A narcissist might try to convince others of their love for their children through grand gestures, such as buying expensive gifts or organizing trips to special places like Disneyland. However, these superficial gestures cannot compensate for the lack of consistent and genuine commitment. Real parenting goes beyond sporadic moments of joy; it requires daily involvement, which includes listening, managing emotions, and being present during difficult times.

Narcissists, however, can hardly be good parents. Their inability to regulate their own emotions and show empathy makes it impossible for them to be meaningfully present for their children. Parenting becomes a performance, a way to gain approval and attention from others, rather than a true commitment to the child's well-being.

Take, for example, a "Disneyland dad" or a "Disneyland mom." These narcissistic parents only show up during fun and leisure moments, when they can easily elicit positive responses from their children. However, when it comes to facing daily challenges like changing diapers, waking up at night to soothe the child, or handling tantrums, the narcissistic parent is completely absent. This lack of consistency and commitment shows that their role as a parent is only partially and dysfunctionally fulfilled.

As a result, the non-narcissistic parent has to take on the role of both parents, becoming a sort of "double parent." This means shouldering all the responsibilities, both physical and emotional, that should be shared. While the narcissistic parent enjoys only the moments of glory, the non-narcissistic parent is forced to handle everything else, including emotional support and daily care.

The truth is, a narcissist does not genuinely love their children. The image of the perfect parent they try to project is merely a facade. The proof lies in their absence when it comes to doing the real work of parenting. When it comes to putting in the real effort to raise a child, the narcissist fails every time. This lack of commitment not only disappoints the partner but also deeply traumatizes the children.

Children of narcissistic parents grow up in an environment of emotional abandonment and abuse. Their self-esteem is constantly undermined, and they often feel like a burden or objects to be used for the narcissist's advantage. This type of psychological abuse has devastating effects on a child's emotional development and creates scars that can last a lifetime.

Narcissists can hardly be good parents because they lack the fundamental qualities needed to raise a child healthily. Their inability to offer genuine love, understanding, and emotional support makes it impossible for them to adequately fulfill the role of a parent. Their behavior, based on selfishness and manipulation, ends up causing deep and lasting damage to their children.

Chapter 2:
Different Types of Narcissistic Parents

In this chapter, we will explore six subtypes of narcissism and their impact on parenting:

1. The Grandiose Narcissist

2. The Malignant Narcissist

3. The Covert Narcissist

4. The Communal Narcissist

5. The Neglectful Narcissist

6. The Self-Righteous Narcissist

Each subtype presents unique challenges for both children and co-parents. Understanding these differences is essential for developing effective strategies to address and mitigate the negative effects of narcissism on the family.

The Grandiose Narcissist

The grandiose narcissist is perhaps the most recognizable type of narcissist. This type is characterized by exaggerated and ostentatious behavior, constantly seeking attention and admiration. When a grandiose narcissist becomes a parent, their parenting style reflects their need to showcase themselves and their family.

Grandiose narcissists are known for being arrogant and self-centered. Their priority is always appearance over substance. For them, being a parent becomes an opportunity to show others how fantastic and perfect they are. They are often described as "Disneyland" parents because they prefer to be present only for big occasions—those that offer an opportunity to show off—rather than for the daily and demanding responsibilities of parenting. They love being the center of attention with their children in photos and in public, but in private, they often lack interest in the day-to-day tasks and needs of their children.

These parents may push their children excessively to excel in activities that make the parent look good, such as sports, school, or other performances. If the child does not meet the grandiose narcissistic parent's expectations, they may be ignored or devalued because the child is seen as an extension of the narcissist rather than as an autonomous individual. Frustration and anger are common reactions when things don't go as desired, as these parents do not tolerate disappointment well.

If you are co-parenting with a grandiose narcissist, it can be shocking and frustrating to see how your ex-partner makes everything revolve around themselves. They constantly talk about what great parents they are and how much they love their kids, but they are not willing to engage in the daily responsibilities of parenting. In the post-divorce period, a grandiose narcissist may seem interested in the children only when it is convenient for them. For example, they may show interest in the children when they want to start a new relationship or live their "new best life," but consider the children an inconvenience when they don't fit into their plans. This can leave you with the less pleasant and more demanding tasks of parenting, such as being the "homework police" or taking care of daily needs.

In summary, the grandiose narcissist uses parenting as a stage to showcase their image, often neglecting the real needs of their children. This type of behavior can have profound and lasting effects on the children, negatively impacting their self-esteem and their ability to form healthy and balanced relationships.

The Malignant Narcissist

The malignant narcissist represents a particularly insidious and dangerous type of narcissism. These individuals are characterized by manipulative, exploitative, and sometimes paranoid behaviors. They can be deceitful and sadistic, creating a family environment filled with fear and tension. For a malignant narcissist, parenting is not about the well-being of the children, but rather about control and domination.

During the divorce process, malignant narcissists can make separation extremely traumatic and complex. They use the legal system to punish their ex-partner, manipulating custody arrangements and financial issues. This constant resort to litigation is a tactic to maintain control and influence over the ex-spouse, prolonging conflict and instability.

In the context of parenting, malignant narcissists are often cold and distant. They can be frightening parents, with children living in a constant state of anxiety. These parents are more interested in power than affection, and their rigid expectations can lead to abusive behaviors. They are often impulsive and careless about their children's safety and well-being, failing to provide a secure family environment.

If you are co-parenting with a malignant narcissist, your experience is likely characterized by extreme exhaustion and concern. The separation may have been particularly difficult and frightening, and your anxiety about your children's safety is a constant worry. Malignant narcissists can be negligent in terms of safety, failing to properly lock doors or ensure a secure environment for the children. Additionally, you might still be subject to threats and intimidating behavior from your ex-partner, making it hard to feel safe and protected.

Children of malignant narcissists may exhibit symptoms similar to those of post-traumatic stress disorder (PTSD). These children grow up in an environment of fear and uncertainty, which can have lasting effects on their mental health and their ability to establish secure and trusting relationships. Even as adults, they may remain hypervigilant and on edge, struggling to feel safe in relationships.

Parenting with a malignant narcissist is an immense challenge. These individuals are not only uninterested in the well-being of their children but may actively seek to use the children as tools to continue exerting control and inflicting emotional harm on their ex-partner. Creating a safe and stable environment for the children in these circumstances requires tremendous effort and attention from the non-narcissistic parent.

The Covert Narcissist

The covert narcissist represents a more subtle and less visible form of narcissism. This type of narcissist tends to present themselves as a victim, exhibiting vulnerable and self-pitying behavior. They constantly feel dissatisfied with their life and believe that nothing ever goes their way. This perception of being a victim of life is reflected in their parenting style as well.

Covert narcissists often inappropriately share their sense of victimhood with their children, who can feel confused and guilty as they try to help or rescue the parent. Children do not fully understand the narcissistic dynamic and seek to alleviate the parent's suffering, taking on emotional responsibilities that should not be theirs. This manipulative behavior leads the children to feel constantly obligated to support and comfort the narcissistic parent.

If you are co-parenting with a covert narcissist, it probably feels like you have another child to care for, rather than an adult partner. Covert narcissists often behave like sulky, complaining teenagers, unable to handle parenting responsibilities. You might find yourself in the position of having to "prepare" them to take care of their own children, as they feel overwhelmed and victimized by circumstances. They alternate between moments of anger and frustration towards the children and moments of self-pity, claiming they are doing their best without receiving any support.

This erratic and manipulative behavior can leave children in a state of constant emotional confusion, alternating between the desire to help the parent and frustration over their inability to manage responsibilities. Children may grow up feeling responsible for their parent's well-being and develop a sense of guilt for not being able to improve the situation.

The covert narcissist uses their victim position to emotionally manipulate the children and co-parent. This dynamic creates an unstable family environment filled with emotional tensions, where children are forced to parent their own parent. Dealing with co-parenting with a covert narcissist requires great care to protect the emotional well-being of the children, ensuring they do not take on inappropriate responsibilities and develop a sense of self-esteem and autonomy.

The Communal Narcissist

The communal narcissist is someone who gains validation through charitable or kind-hearted actions. These individuals want to be seen as humanitarians or saviors, constantly seeking the spotlight for their good deeds. They use social media and other platforms to show the world how dedicated they are to helping others. However, this apparent dedication to the community often does not translate into their behavior within the family.

Behind closed doors, the communal narcissist can be detached and uninterested in their own children. While they may be enthusiastic about helping children in other parts of the world or children not related to them through charitable initiatives, they often show a lack of engagement with their own children. They love to showcase their role as parents for a photo or a public occasion but are not willing to commit to the daily responsibilities that parenting entails.

These parents may make their children feel like tools to enhance their public image. The children might wonder why their parent dedicates so much energy and attention to helping others but not them. This can lead to a sense of confusion and inadequacy in the children, who might feel they are not important enough to deserve their parent's attention.

If you are co-parenting with a communal narcissist, you might find yourself having to manage around their "important" work of saving the world. They might demand the children's presence for public events, photographs, or occasions where they can be seen as devoted parents. However, when they do not need the children for image purposes, they may be less present and less involved. Additionally, they might expect you and others around them to support their important work, adjusting your schedules to meet their needs.

The disconnect between the public image of the communal narcissist and their private behavior can create a frustrating and destabilizing family environment. The children may grow up feeling secondary to their parent's public causes and develop feelings of resentment or low self-esteem. As a co-parent, it is important to help the children understand that their worth is not determined by the public attention they receive, but by their inherent importance and uniqueness.

The communal narcissist uses their image as a benefactor to gain validation, often at the expense of genuine involvement with their own children. This behavior creates a gap between their public image and private reality, which can have profound and lasting effects on the children. As a co-parent, it is essential to work towards bridging this gap, providing the children with a stable and loving environment where they feel truly valued.

The Neglectful Narcissist

The neglectful narcissist is characterized by an almost total disinterest in the people in their life unless they can offer something useful. They view people as conveniences, using them only when needed. When it comes to parenting, neglectful narcissists see their children as a major inconvenience and, as a result, are often detached and disinterested.

These parents are cold, distant, and remote, with limited interest in their children. Children who grow up with a neglectful narcissistic parent often desperately seek their parent's attention, ultimately feeling unworthy of love. This behavior can have devastating effects on the children's self-esteem, leading them to believe they are not important enough to deserve their parent's attention and love.

If you are co-parenting with a neglectful narcissist, your primary task will likely be helping your children understand and overcome the crisis of feeling unloved or unwanted by their parent. The neglectful narcissist might decide to cut ties and leave the children entirely to you, forcing you to take on all the responsibilities. This scenario can be extremely painful for the children, who not only face a lack of attention from one parent but also the sense of abandonment.

Children raised by a neglectful narcissistic parent may develop a sense of "not enough," feeling as if they have to jump through hoops to get attention from others. They might adopt hobbies or interests just to try to get a bit of interaction with the neglectful parent. This dynamic affects not only their childhood but can also lead to difficulties in adult relationships, where they continue to seek the approval and attention they never received as children.

The neglectful narcissist creates a cold and detached family environment where children struggle for attention and love. This type of narcissism can lead to a deep sense of insecurity and low self-esteem in the children, who may grow up feeling inadequate. As a co-parent, it is crucial to provide your children with a loving and attentive environment, helping them develop a sense of self-worth and understand that their importance does not depend on the attention received from the neglectful parent.

The Self-Righteous Narcissist

The self-righteous narcissist gains their validation and sense of superiority by maintaining a facade of impeccable morality and righteousness. These individuals see themselves as morally superior and tend to judge and criticize others harshly. They are obsessed with rules and doing things "the right way" rather than with a more flexible and loving approach that would be better suited to children.

These parents may seem very loyal and are often seen as pillars of the religious community or devoted followers of a strict moral code. However, this apparent righteousness hides a rigidity and authoritarianism that can be extremely damaging to their children. Self-righteous narcissists are often critical of everything and everyone, including their children, creating an environment of constant judgment and unrealistic expectations.

Children raised by self-righteous parents may feel that love is conditional on adhering to the rules and moral principles set by their parents. This can lead to an extremely restrictive and severe childhood, where children feel they must constantly prove their worth to be loved. This type of parenting can generate a strong sense of shame and self-judgment in the children, who may grow up feeling trapped between the desire to conform and the urge to rebel against these rigid expectations.

If you are co-parenting with a self-righteous narcissist, be prepared to argue over every minor financial issue and to endure constant criticism about how you run your household. These individuals can be extremely ritualistic and obsessive about trivial details and may fight for even a few extra minutes of custody if they feel the rules have

39

not been followed to the letter. This attitude can make co-parenting an exhausting and frustrating experience.

Children may find themselves having to navigate between a rigidly regulated home environment and a more flexible and loving one, creating a dissonance that can be difficult to manage. They might adapt their behavior depending on which parent they are with, leading to a sense of confusion and insecurity.

In summary, the self-righteous narcissist maintains a facade of morality and righteousness that masks a critical and rigid nature. This type of parenting can lead to a harsh childhood for children, forced to conform to unrealistic standards to gain their parent's love and approval. As a co-parent, it is crucial to create an environment where your children feel loved and accepted for who they are, helping them develop healthy self-esteem and a balanced view of life.

Chapter 3:
6 Approaches of Co-Parenting with a Narcissist

Facing co-parenting with a narcissistic ex-partner is one of the toughest challenges a parent can encounter. The complex and often toxic dynamics of a narcissistic relationship do not disappear once the relationship ends; in fact, they tend to intensify when children are involved. The range of behaviors and attitudes that parents adopt in these situations is broad and often influenced by their understanding of narcissism and the experience they have gained over time.

In this chapter, we will explore various ways of co-parenting with a narcissist, based on observations and patterns identified over the years. Every parent might see themselves in one or more of these approaches, and as we will see, these strategies can evolve as one gains more awareness and understanding of narcissism. Whether it involves fighting for custody, managing one's mental health, or finding a balance between justice and realism, the goal is to provide useful tools to protect both your children and yourself, while ensuring a more stable and serene environment.

The Lion/Lioness Parent

Imagine being in a fierce battle, fighting for what is dearest to your heart: your children. This is the reality for many parents facing divorce or separation with a narcissistic partner. The desire to protect one's children from toxic influences is natural and understandable. However, in this context, being a combative parent, like a lion or a lioness, can lead to unexpected and often harmful consequences.

Many parents, as soon as the legal battle begins, openly declare their intention to fight vigorously for custody of their children. This attitude, though motivated by love and protection, can be a grave mistake. Narcissistic parents are shrewd manipulators and use any information to their advantage. Showing your determination and desire to obtain full custody can become a weakness that the narcissist will exploit.

The narcissist may not initially be interested in primary custody of the children. Some of them see the children as mere tools for gaining social approval or punishing the ex-partner. However, once they understand how important custody is to you, the narcissist may suddenly decide to fight fiercely for it, not out of love for the children, but to gain leverage against you.

This dynamic turns the legal battle into a war of emotional attrition. The narcissist, fueled by revenge, will use every tactic available to prolong and complicate the process, forcing you into increasing legal expenses and emotional exhaustion. The result is that, in the end, you may find yourself having to accept painful compromises or losing sight of your main goal: the well-being of your children.

So, how can you fight this battle without falling into the narcissist's traps? The answer lies in strategy and discretion. It is crucial to remain calm and not openly show your intentions. Externally, you might appear more flexible and less determined, thus reducing the narcissist's desire to fight you just for the sake of it. This does not mean abandoning the fight for your children, but tackling it with cunning and preparation.

For example, you can gather detailed evidence and documentation of the narcissist's actions without revealing your moves. Speak with your lawyer confidentially, planning each step carefully. The key is not to let the narcissist understand how crucial obtaining custody is for you. You might even consider showing apparent disinterest in some aspects of the process, thus misleading the narcissist and reducing their motivation to fight you.

Ultimately, being a lion or lioness parent does not necessarily mean always showing strength and readiness for battle. True strength lies in the ability to handle the situation with intelligence and cunning, protecting your children without exposing them to further conflicts and traumas. This approach requires a delicate balance between internal determination and external strategy, but it is essential to prevent the narcissist from using your own children as weapons in their personal war against you.

Remember, the battle for your children's custody is not just a legal matter but also an issue of emotional survival. Keep your focus on what truly matters: your children's well-being and stability. With the right strategy and adequate support, you can navigate through these turbulent waters and emerge victorious, protecting what you love most.

The Depressed and Hopeless Parent

For many parents, the end of a relationship with a narcissistic partner marks the peak of years of emotional destabilization, dehumanization, and exhaustion. Facing a legal battle for child custody can seem insurmountable, especially for those who have already suffered the devastating effects of a narcissistic relationship.

These parents often feel overwhelmed and unable to continue fighting. The sense of powerlessness is amplified by the daily challenges of raising children in a context of constant tension and conflict. If there is a history of mental health issues, such as depression, the relationship with a narcissist can significantly worsen these conditions, making it almost impossible to handle the legal and emotional difficulties of a divorce.

The divorce process and custody negotiations can be exhausting. Courts, often inattentive to the dynamics of narcissistic abuse, may seem indifferent to the parent's suffering. Frustration and despair increase when the needs of the children are ignored or minimized. In this scenario, the parent may feel pressured to give in, accepting unfavorable custody or divorce agreements just to end the torment.

However, it is essential that these parents do not succumb to despair. Psychological support is crucial and non-negotiable. Therapy not only provides a safe space to process pain and frustration but is also essential for maintaining the clarity and strength needed to continue fighting. A therapist can help develop effective coping strategies, strengthen self-esteem, and establish a support network crucial for facing legal and emotional battles.

The biggest risk for the depressed and hopeless parent is giving up completely, allowing the narcissist to gain greater control over the children. This not only compromises the well-being of the parent but also exposes the children to further abuse and manipulation. It is vital to remember that even in the darkest moments, giving in to despair is not the solution. Seeking and accepting help is a sign of strength, not weakness.

Additionally, the narcissist may exploit the parent's depression to build a negative narrative in court, claiming that the other parent is unable to care for the children. This is another reason why psychological support is vital: it demonstrates to the courts that the parent is actively addressing their difficulties and working to improve their situation and that of their children.

For these parents, participating in support groups specifically for victims of narcissistic abuse can be extremely helpful. Sharing experiences with others who have gone through similar situations helps to not feel alone and to find new strategies for dealing with difficulties. Hearing success stories from others can offer hope and inspiration, showing that it is possible to emerge from the narcissist's shadow and rebuild a more stable and happy life.

Finally, self-care is essential. Even if it seems impossible to find time for oneself amidst the chaos, dedicating time to physical and emotional well-being is crucial. Activities like physical exercise, meditation, and carving out moments of tranquility can make a big difference in the long run.

Facing a divorce and a custody battle with a narcissistic partner is one of the most difficult challenges imaginable. However, with the right support and a strong safety net, it is possible to overcome even the toughest moments. Depression and the feeling of powerlessness should not define your ability to be a good parent. With time, support, and determination, you can find the strength to fight for yourself and your children, ensuring them a more serene and secure future.

The Injustice Fighter Parent

Engaging in a legal battle against a narcissistic partner can quickly become an endless nightmare. The parent who tries to fight every perceived injustice, whether financial, custodial, or otherwise, risks falling into a spiral of frustration and mounting expenses. This approach, although motivated by a legitimate sense of justice, can become a dangerous trap.

Many parents in this situation feel the need to meticulously document every wrong they have suffered. Every violation, missed payment, and inappropriate behavior is recorded in the hope of presenting a strong case in court. However, this behavior can lead to an endless cycle of gathering evidence and returning to court, with skyrocketing legal costs and devastating emotional tolls.

One of the most common mistakes is failing to radically accept the reality of the situation. Family courts often do not fully recognize or care about the injustices raised by parents facing narcissistic ex-partners. This perceived injustice can fuel a sense of indignation and the desire to keep fighting, but the reality is that complete justice is rarely achieved.

The parent who relentlessly pursues justice may find themselves dedicating an incredible amount of time and resources to this battle. Every documentation, every hearing, every new lawyer represents another step in an endless marathon. This not only drains financial resources but also distracts from the need to heal and build a stable life for the children.

Another significant risk is becoming trapped in a cycle of never-ending legal battles. Every new perceived injustice becomes a reason to return to court, keeping the parent tied to a system that offers no definitive resolutions. This cycle can become the parent's full-time job, preventing any possibility of recovery and progress.

It's important to remember that narcissists often derive pleasure from conflict and fighting. Continuing to battle can give the narcissist exactly what they want: an opportunity to maintain control and inflict further pain. The relentless fight for justice can, paradoxically, fuel the cycle of abuse and manipulation.

The injustice fighter parent must learn to choose their battles wisely. Not every injustice needs to be fought to the end. Sometimes, accepting a compromise, however painful, can be the wisest strategy to protect one's mental health and the well-being of the children. Accepting that the judicial system will not always deliver complete justice is a crucial step towards healing.

Radical acceptance means recognizing the limitations of the legal system and the realities of narcissism. This doesn't mean giving up but rather facing the situation with realism and pragmatism. It means understanding that not all battles can be won and that sometimes it is better to conserve one's energy for the most important issues.

To break free from this spiral, it is essential to have good legal support that understands the dynamics of narcissism and can offer strategic advice on which battles are worth fighting. Additionally, seeking therapeutic support to manage frustration and the sense of injustice can help maintain a balanced perspective and avoid emotional exhaustion.

Ultimately, the parent who tries to fight every injustice must learn to balance the desire for justice with practical reality. Focusing on battles that have a real and significant impact on the children's well-being and on their own emotional and financial stability is crucial to emerging victorious from this challenge. With time, adequate support, and a well-thought-out strategy, it is possible to navigate the pitfalls of divorcing a narcissist and build a more serene and secure life for oneself and one's children.

The Indifferent Parent

The indifferent parent is often the result of years of exhaustion caused by a narcissistic relationship. After countless emotional and legal battles, indifference can seem like a natural response. However, this apparent apathy can carry significant risks, both for the parent and the children.

Indifference can stem from a sort of emotional burnout. After years of abuse and manipulation, some parents develop a form of self-defense that leads them to emotionally detach from conflicting situations. This attitude does not necessarily mean a lack of love or concern for the children, but rather a survival mechanism to cope with the unbearable.

In some cases, indifference can be a form of karmic acceptance, a letting go of events with the belief that every effort is in vain. This fatalistic view of the situation can be dangerous as it leads to missing important strategic opportunities to improve one's legal standing and the well-being of the children.

Being indifferent can mean missing crucial chances to adequately prepare for legal battles. Even if the judicial system may seem unfair and inadequate in dealing with narcissists, it is still essential to remain vigilant and prepared. Neglecting this aspect can lead to unfavorable legal decisions that will have a lasting impact on the children.

Indifference should not be confused with depression. Although there are overlaps, the indifferent parent might not be clinically depressed but simply have developed a detached attitude as a response to years of abuse. However, this state of apathy can be perceived by the courts as disinterest or an inability to care for the children, feeding into the narcissist's narrative.

For many parents, indifference is a response to the feeling of futility in their efforts. After repeated failed attempts to achieve justice, continuing to fight can seem pointless. However, it is important to remember that every small step forward counts and can make a significant difference in the long run.

A strategic approach is fundamental. Even if the indifferent parent feels overwhelmed, it is essential to find the strength to actively participate in the legal battle. This means working closely with a lawyer who understands the dynamics of narcissism and can provide advice on which battles are worth fighting. Additionally, keeping accurate documentation and preparing thoroughly for hearings can make a significant difference.

Another crucial aspect is psychological support. Even if the indifferent parent may not feel depressed, therapy can help manage emotional detachment and find new motivations to continue fighting. The support of a therapist can help develop effective coping strategies and maintain a balanced perspective.

Participating in support groups for parents facing similar situations can be very helpful. Sharing experiences with others who have gone through the same challenges helps to feel less alone and find new resources to tackle difficulties. Indifference can be overcome with the right support and a strong safety net.

Ultimately, indifference should not define the parent. While it may seem like a natural response to the exhaustion caused by a narcissistic relationship, it is important to find ways to remain involved and active in the fight for the children's well-being. With the right support and a well-thought-out strategy, it is possible to turn indifference into positive and constructive action, ensuring a more secure and stable future for oneself and one's children.

The Strategic Parent

The strategic parent seeks to balance the desire for justice with the practical realities of dealing with a narcissistic ex-partner. Understanding the dynamics of narcissism, the limitations of the legal system, and the importance of thorough preparation are key elements of this approach.

Strategic parents are aware that narcissists often use children as tools for manipulation and control. Reacting impulsively to provocations can give the narcissist an advantage. Therefore, maintaining a calm and rational demeanor throughout the process is crucial. This awareness helps navigate the legal landscape more effectively.

Meticulous preparation is essential. Strategic parents document every interaction with the narcissist, collecting concrete evidence to use in court. Recording conversations, saving emails and text messages, and keeping a detailed diary of visits and interactions are all fundamental practices. Such documentation not only serves as a defense against false accusations but also demonstrates the parent's reliability and stability.

Collaborating with a lawyer experienced in narcissistic dynamics is another key element. Not all attorneys understand the nuances of narcissistic abuse, so it is essential to find a legal professional who can offer strategic advice on how to handle the case. A competent lawyer can make the difference between a favorable judgment and one that leaves the parent and children in a vulnerable position.

Radical acceptance is a central concept for the strategic parent. It means recognizing that the legal system might not fully acknowledge the injustices suffered and that complete justice might be unattainable. This doesn't mean giving up on one's rights, but rather approaching the situation pragmatically. For example, accepting a compromise in terms of custody might offer greater stability and security for the children in the long term.

Being strategic also means knowing when to choose your battles. Not every injustice needs to be contested in court. Sometimes, it is wiser to focus on what has a direct and significant impact on the children's lives. This approach not only conserves emotional and financial resources but also shows the court that the parent is balanced and child-focused.

Psychological support is crucial for strategic parents. Therapy helps develop effective coping strategies, strengthen self-esteem, and provide a safe space to process emotional difficulties. Children can also benefit from psychological support, helping them navigate the complexities of family dynamics with a narcissistic parent.

Community support can also make a significant difference. Joining support groups for parents facing similar situations provides a sense of belonging and understanding. Sharing experiences and strategies with other parents can offer new perspectives and practical solutions.

The ultimate goal of the strategic parent is not just to win a legal battle but to ensure a stable and secure future for themselves and their children. This requires a combination of thorough preparation, collaboration with experienced professionals, radical acceptance, and emotional support. With time, patience, and a well-thought-out strategy, it is possible to overcome the challenges posed by a narcissistic ex-partner and build a more serene and fulfilling life for oneself and one's children.

Embracing Change and Finding Strength

After exploring the different ways of co-parenting with a narcissist, it's important to remember that these categories are not static. It's not just about identifying your current approach but understanding that evolution and adaptation are possible over time. As you gain a deeper awareness of narcissism and develop new strategies, your method of co-parenting can significantly change.

Parents may start with a combative attitude, like that of a lion or lioness, but over time, they might find that a more strategic and discreet approach is more effective. Others might go through phases of despair and helplessness, only to find strength and hope again through psychological support and community connections.

Recognizing the potential for growth and adaptation is essential. With a better understanding of narcissism and new strategies, you can transform how you handle co-parenting. Legal and emotional support, along with community solidarity, plays a fundamental role in this transformative journey.

Accepting that the legal system may not always deliver complete justice is an important step. However, by approaching the situation pragmatically and with thorough preparation, it's possible to protect your children and ensure a more stable and secure future for them. Every small step forward, every daily victory, contributes to building a better life for you and your children.

Never underestimate the importance of support. Joining support groups, seeking help from specialized therapists, and connecting with other parents in similar situations can make a huge difference. These resources offer not only practical strategies but also comfort and hope.

In the end, co-parenting with a narcissist is a long and arduous journey, but you are not alone. With time, patience, and the right support, you can not only survive this experience but emerge stronger and more resilient. It's a journey of personal growth and protecting your children, where every step forward is a victory towards a more serene and fulfilling future.

So, whether you feel like a fighting lion, a parent overwhelmed by despair, or are striving to be strategic, remember that your ability to adapt and grow is your greatest strength. Continue to fight for what's right for you and your children, and always seek the support you need to move forward. With determination and resilience, you can overcome the challenges and build a better future for your family.

Chapter 4:
The Truth You Can't Share with Your Kids

The Importance of Not Speaking Badly of the Narcissistic Parent

When it comes to co-parenting, the unanimous advice is clear: never speak ill of the other parent to the children. This principle, valid in any context of separation or divorce, becomes even more crucial when the other parent is a narcissist. But why? And how difficult is it to follow this rule?

The truth is that children are like sponges: they absorb everything they see and hear. Hearing one parent speak badly of the other creates an internal conflict within them, a cognitive dissonance that can have long-term effects on their emotional and mental health. This principle is based on the idea that children need to love both parents without feeling guilty or divided in their loyalty.

However, when the other parent is a narcissist, the situation becomes even more complicated. Narcissists are skilled manipulators and can present themselves to the children as affectionate and playful parents while behind the scenes, they inflict emotional and psychological abuse on their partner. This behavior creates a distorted and confusing image for the children, who see one parent as "perfect" and the other constantly stressed and unhappy.

The task of the abused parent is arduous: to remain calm, not to speak ill of the other parent, and not to justify the other parent's negative behaviors. It is a delicate and exhausting balance that requires immense inner strength.

For example, imagine a mother who sees her ex-partner, the narcissist, treating their children like little kings during visitation time, taking them to amusement parks, buying them expensive gifts, and doing everything possible to appear as the perfect parent. When the children come home, they excitedly recount their adventures while she, who lives daily under the weight of abuse and manipulation, must smile and hide her pain. She must listen, support their stories, and suppress the urge to tell the truth. This creates enormous internal tension, a knot of conflicting emotions that is hard to untangle.

But what is the alternative? Speaking ill of the narcissistic parent to the children might seem like a temporary relief, but in the long run, it would only create further division and confusion. Children, in fact, do not have the emotional maturity to fully understand the complexity of narcissistic abuse dynamics. Telling them the truth about a parent might make them feel betrayed and forced to choose sides, a responsibility too great for them to bear.

The solution, although difficult to accept, is to maintain a neutral position. The abused parent must find their support elsewhere: in trusted friends, a therapist, or support groups. This not only helps to maintain the emotional stability necessary to raise the children but also avoids burdening the children with emotional weight they should not have to carry.

The Paradox of the Narcissist Parent

Narcissists are masters at creating a double reality. On one hand, they can be charming, fun, and seemingly devoted to their children. On the other hand, they inflict psychological abuse and manipulation on their partner, creating a toxic home environment. This contrast between the two faces of the narcissist is particularly harmful to children, who struggle to reconcile the image of the affectionate parent with that of the abusive person.

54

Imagine being a child who sees their narcissistic parent behaving exemplary in front of others: organizing parties, actively participating in their school life, and showing affection in public. However, behind closed doors, the same parent can become critical, manipulative, and insensitive. This inconsistent behavior not only confuses children but also forces them to live in a state of constant anxiety and uncertainty.

Narcissists are incredibly skilled at creating an image of perfection. They can be extremely attentive to details when it comes to showcasing their best side. For example, a narcissistic father might spend entire days organizing fun activities with the children, taking pictures, and posting them on social media to show everyone how "dedicated" he is. These images of public happiness can mask a very different reality made up of control and emotional manipulation.

This double facade is a deliberate strategy by the narcissist to maintain control and manipulate others' perceptions. For children, this alternation between love and cruelty is particularly devastating. They might begin to doubt their own feelings and perceptions, wondering why the other parent always seems stressed and unhappy while the narcissist appears perfect.

The abused parent, aware of the true nature of the narcissistic partner, faces the difficult challenge of not openly exposing the other parent to the children. This requires considerable inner strength and the ability to manage one's emotions. It is crucial for the abused parent to find ways to protect their children without further damaging their perception of either parent.

For instance, if a child expresses excitement about something the narcissistic parent did, the abused parent can respond with empathy and support, without trying to diminish or negate the positive experience. This approach helps maintain a sense of stability for the child, even if it can be extremely painful for the abused parent.

In the context of co-parenting, it is essential for the abused parent to find a balance between protecting the children and maintaining a certain level of neutrality. This also means being ready to respond with honesty but delicacy when the children start noticing discrepancies in the narcissistic parent's behavior.

Another example could be a child asking why the narcissistic parent gets angry easily. In such cases, the abused parent can explain that sometimes people have difficulty managing their emotions and that it is not the child's fault. This type of response helps protect the child's self-esteem without demonizing the other parent.

Ultimately, the paradox of the narcissistic parent requires the abused parent to navigate a sea of contradictions, staying calm and protecting their children from the emotional waves created by the other parent. This delicate balance is essential to ensure that the children grow up in an environment that is as serene and safe as possible.

The Impact on Children

The contradictory and manipulative behaviors of a narcissistic parent can profoundly affect children. These children are often forced to navigate feelings of guilt, shame, and confusion as they try to relate to both parents. The presence of a narcissistic parent creates an unstable environment where children must constantly adapt to mood and behavior changes.

Imagine a child who sees their narcissistic parent alternating between moments of extreme affection and outbursts of anger or indifference. This alternation not only confuses them but can also lead them to doubt their own perception of reality. Children might start to wonder if they are the cause of the narcissistic parent's negative behaviors, developing a sense of guilt and inadequacy.

Additionally, children can feel torn in their loyalty. On one hand, they want to love and respect both parents; on the other, they witness the harmful actions of the narcissistic parent. This division can create deep internal conflict, making children feel they must choose sides, an emotionally devastating task.

The abused parent, trying to protect the children from the negative influence of the narcissist, faces the challenge of maintaining open and honest communication without denigrating the other parent. For example, if a child expresses discomfort about the narcissistic parent's behavior, the abused parent can validate the child's feelings without adding further criticism. This helps the child feel understood and supported without feeling forced to take a stance against the other parent.

Another critical aspect is the impact on the children's self-esteem. Growing up with a narcissistic parent can negatively affect their self-perception, as the narcissist tends to use the children as tools to fulfill their need for control and validation. Children may grow up feeling constantly judged and never good enough to meet the narcissistic parent's expectations.

The abused parent must work to build and reinforce the children's self-esteem. This can include encouraging their passions and interests, celebrating their successes, big or small, and creating a home environment where the children feel safe and loved for who they are, not for what they do.

It's essential for the abused parent to recognize signs of stress and anxiety in the children and help them develop effective coping strategies. This can include practicing relaxing activities, engaging in hobbies they enjoy, and, if necessary, seeking professional support such as a child therapist.

As we continue exploring the dynamics of co-parenting with a narcissist, it's clear that the emotional well-being of the children must be a top priority. Protecting the children from the negative effects of narcissistic behavior requires constant effort and a great deal of patience and love.

Challenges for the Abused Parent

One of the main challenges for the abused parent is managing the dichotomy between the public image and the private reality of the narcissistic parent. The narcissist skillfully manipulates others' perceptions, presenting themselves as the ideal parent while constantly undermining the efforts of the other parent. This can lead the abused parent to feel isolated and frustrated.

It's important to develop strategies to handle this situation. For instance, keeping a detailed journal of interactions with the narcissist can be helpful. This journal can document manipulative and abusive behaviors, providing a clear and detailed account that can be useful in legal or therapeutic contexts.

Additionally, finding ways to strengthen autonomy and self-esteem is crucial. The abused parent can engage in activities that promote personal and professional growth. Taking courses, developing new skills, or pursuing hobbies can help build greater self-confidence, regardless of the narcissist's criticisms.

Another significant challenge is protecting the children from the negative influences of the narcissistic parent. Instead of downplaying the positive experiences the children may have with the narcissist, the abused parent can focus on teaching critical thinking skills. For example, helping children recognize manipulative behaviors and express their feelings in a healthy way can enhance their ability to handle difficult situations.

When children report concerning behaviors of the narcissistic parent, the abused parent can use these moments as teaching opportunities. Explaining why certain behaviors are unacceptable and offering alternatives on how to handle such situations in the future can be very helpful.

Finally, it is essential for the abused parent to find ways to take care of their own mental and physical health. Practices like meditation, regular exercise, and relaxation techniques can help manage stress. In times of particular difficulty, exploring resources such as books, podcasts, and articles on similar experiences can provide new perspectives and strategies.

These concrete actions can help the abused parent navigate the complex dynamics of co-parenting with a narcissist, protecting themselves and their children.

The Temptation to Tell the Truth to the Children

When living in a relationship with a narcissistic partner, the temptation to reveal the truth about the other parent's behavior to the children can be strong. However, this decision is complex and fraught with implications.

For many abused parents, the urge to expose the narcissistic parent's true nature comes from a desire to protect the children and prevent them from seeing manipulative behavior as normal or acceptable. This reaction is understandable, but the consequences of such a revelation can be harmful.

The truth can be heavy for children, who may not have the emotional maturity to fully comprehend it. Telling children that one of their parents is a narcissist could make them feel divided and forced to choose between the two parents. Additionally, it could lead them to develop feelings of guilt or responsibility for the situation.

The key to handling this temptation lies in communication. Instead of revealing everything, the abused parent can adopt a gradual and strategic approach. For example, they can explain to the children that everyone makes mistakes and sometimes people behave in ways we don't fully understand. This type of dialogue can help children develop a more nuanced understanding of family dynamics without feeling overwhelmed.

An effective method to help children understand complex situations is the use of storytelling. Telling stories that address themes of justice, integrity, and resilience can offer children models of positive behavior without necessarily exposing the details of the family situation.

It is crucial to create an environment where children feel safe expressing their emotions and concerns. The abused parent can encourage the children to openly talk about their feelings, responding with empathy and support. This approach helps build a trustful bond and reduces the confusion and anxiety that children may feel.

Teaching children to recognize and manage their own emotions is essential. This process includes identifying emotions, learning stress management techniques, and practicing assertive communication. These skills help children better navigate complex family dynamics and develop greater emotional resilience.

The abused parent can become a positive role model for the children. Demonstrating how to handle conflicts calmly and respectfully, taking care of oneself, and maintaining personal integrity in difficult situations are valuable lessons that children can learn by observing.

Sometimes, involving a neutral third party, such as a family therapist, can be helpful. A professional can offer a balanced perspective and provide strategies for managing emotions and improving family communication.

Handling the temptation to tell the truth to the children requires a delicate and strategic approach. Protecting the children from negative dynamics while helping them develop a balanced and resilient understanding of reality is a complex but essential task.

Managing Guilt and Remorse

Guilt is a common emotion for parents who face co-parenting with a narcissistic partner. They blame themselves for not recognizing the warning signs in time or for the negative experiences their children have to endure. However, it is essential to understand that these decisions were made with the best intentions and with the information available at the time.

Overcoming these feelings requires a mindful and compassionate approach toward oneself. Reflecting on the circumstances that led to the relationship helps in understanding one's actions and motivations better. Recognizing that no one is perfect and that everyone makes mistakes is a crucial step in freeing oneself from guilt. Accepting one's imperfections allows for moving forward with greater serenity.

Learning more about narcissism and toxic relationships not only helps in better understanding the past but also provides practical tools to better manage the present and future. Knowledge is a powerful tool for facing challenges.

Self-compassion is essential for managing remorse. Treating oneself with kindness and understanding, as one would a dear friend, is vital. Speaking to oneself with words of comfort and encouragement instead of self-criticism helps to remember that one did their best with the resources available. Practicing mindfulness can be helpful in maintaining a balanced perspective, allowing one to be present in the moment and accept emotions without judgment.

Seeking external support is also crucial. Talking with trusted friends, family, or mental health professionals can offer emotional support and new perspectives. A solid support system can make a significant difference during difficult times.

Despite the challenges, it is fundamental to recognize one's strength and the positive role one plays in their children's lives. Being a solid and present parent is crucial for their well-being. Children who have at least one stable and affectionate parent can develop a sense of security and self-esteem, even in the face of difficulties caused by the narcissistic parent. Demonstrating resilience and the ability to face challenges teaches children valuable lessons about strength and self-worth.

Ensuring that children have a safe space to express their emotions and feel loved is fundamental. Creating a positive and supportive home environment can make a significant difference in their emotional development. Being available to listen to and support children, helping them navigate their experiences with understanding and affection, strengthens the bond and trust.

Chapter 5:
Parental Alienation

Parental alienation is one of the most toxic and devastating phenomena that can occur within a family. When the alienating parent is also a narcissist, the situation becomes even more dramatic and complex. Narcissistic parental alienation not only undermines the relationship between the targeted parent and the child but also creates an environment of manipulation and control that can have long-term consequences for everyone involved.

In general terms, parental alienation involves the psychological manipulation of a child by one parent with the aim of destroying the emotional bond between the child and the other parent. This is achieved through a series of strategies that lead the child to view the other parent as an enemy, deserving of disdain and hatred. When the alienator is a narcissist, these tactics become particularly pernicious. The narcissistic parent is often driven by a desire for revenge, a need to feel superior, and a will to exert total control.

Narcissistic parental alienation manifests through behaviors aimed at diminishing the other parent in the eyes of the child. These behaviors include sending poisonous messages that portray the targeted parent as unloving, unsafe, or unavailable. The child is led to believe that the targeted parent hates them or that the environment in which they live with the targeted parent is dangerous. In this way, the child starts to internalize a distorted view of the targeted parent, who may have been affectionate and present up until that point.

One of the first signs of parental alienation is limited communication. The alienating parent begins to reduce contact between the child and the targeted parent, using excuses such as illness, school commitments, or technical problems. Every pretext is used to prevent the child from spending time with the other parent. This limitation of contact not only damages the relationship between the child and the targeted parent but also increases the control the alienator has over the child.

Another tactic used is to replace and erase the targeted parent from the child's life. The alienating parent might introduce a new partner as the new dad or mom, trying to eliminate all traces of the targeted parent. Phrases like "we don't need the old dad/mom" become common, and the child is encouraged to see the alienator as the only loving and present parent.

Narcissistic parental alienation doesn't stop there. The child is often turned into a sort of spy, tasked with reporting back to the alienating parent about everything that happens in the targeted parent's home. This not only further compromises the trust between the child and the targeted parent but also provides the alienator with more tools for manipulation. Additionally, the authority of the targeted parent is constantly undermined. If the targeted parent sets a rule, the alienating parent contradicts it, reinforcing the idea that the targeted parent is incompetent or irrelevant.

Understanding narcissistic parental alienation is crucial for addressing and mitigating its devastating effects. The first step is recognizing the signs of this manipulation. It is essential to act promptly to protect the child and seek help from professionals experienced in this field. Only with a deep understanding of the problem and quick intervention can there be hope of restoring a healthy and loving environment for the child.

Alienating Parent's Tactics

Recognizing the signs of narcissistic parental alienation is crucial for timely intervention. The indicators of this manipulation can vary, but there are some recurring behaviors that can help identify the situation.

One of the first signs of parental alienation is the sending of poisonous messages to the child about the targeted parent. The alienating parent portrays the targeted parent as unloving, unsafe, absent, or even dangerous. These messages aim to instill a negative and distorted view of the targeted parent in the child, making them believe that the targeted parent is unworthy of their love and trust. This type of psychological manipulation can leave the child feeling confused and insecure, negatively affecting their perception of the targeted parent.

Another indicator is the limitation of contact and communication between the child and the targeted parent. The alienating parent uses every possible excuse to prevent the child from spending time with the other parent. Excuses such as illnesses, school commitments, technical problems, or simply stating that the child does not want to see the other parent are commonly used. This progressive isolation not only damages the bond between the child and the targeted parent but also increases the control the alienating parent has over the child.

Replacing and erasing the targeted parent from the child's life is another common tactic. The alienating parent might introduce a new partner as the new dad or mom, trying to make the child forget about the targeted parent. Phrases like "we don't need the old dad/mom" become recurrent, and the child is encouraged to see the alienating parent as the only loving and present parent. This process of replacement can be extremely painful for the child, who has to renegotiate their family identity.

The alienating parent may also encourage the child to violate the targeted parent's trust. This is done by turning the child into a sort of spy, tasked with reporting back to the alienating parent about everything that happens in the targeted parent's home. Questions like "What happens at dad/mom's house?" or "What did you have for dinner?" become tools to gather information. This behavior not only further compromises the trust between the child and the targeted parent but also provides the alienating parent with more ammunition to manipulate and control the situation.

Finally, the authority of the targeted parent is constantly undermined. If the targeted parent sets a rule, the alienating parent contradicts it, reinforcing the idea that the targeted parent is incompetent or irrelevant. For example, if the targeted parent tells the child they cannot stay out late, the alienating parent will say they can do whatever they want, thus undermining the targeted parent's authority. This type of behavior creates confusion and insecurity in the child, who does not know whom to obey and feels constantly torn in two opposite directions.

These indicators and tactics of narcissistic parental alienation are clear signs of a manipulative situation that requires immediate intervention. Recognizing them is the first step to protecting the child and restoring a healthy and safe family environment. In the next section, we will explore the effects of this manipulation on children and the necessary actions to counteract it effectively.

Effects on Children and Necessary Interventions

Narcissistic parental alienation can have severe consequences on children, profoundly impacting their mental health and emotional well-being. Children who are victims of alienation may develop anxiety, depression, academic problems, and social isolation. This constant manipulation can leave them feeling confused, insecure, and lonely, with long-term effects on their lives.

To effectively address this situation, here are ten practical strategies:

1. Stay Calm

Remaining calm during conflicts is essential to avoid escalating the situation. For example, staying calm during a heated discussion with an ex-spouse in front of the children can help avoid raising voices and demonstrate positive behavior. A parent who chooses not to respond to provocations can focus on the children's well-being, creating a more serene environment.

Practice deep breathing techniques when you feel tension rising to help maintain calm during difficult situations.

2. Express Love

Consistently showing love and support to your children is crucial. Writing a letter to your children each week, expressing love and appreciation for them and the special moments you've shared, can strengthen your bond despite the challenges. Leaving affectionate notes in your child's school bag can also help.

Dedicate time each day for a special moment of affection, such as a hug or a sincere "I love you."

3. Use Positive Language

Using positive language helps create a more peaceful environment. Instead of saying, "I'm sorry you have to spend time with the other parent," try saying, "I hope you have a great time with the other parent." Avoid using negative terms about your ex-spouse during conversations with your children, and focus on the positive aspects of their daily routine.

Create a list of positive phrases to use in daily conversations and commit to using them regularly.

4. Maintain Contact

Maintaining regular communication is essential to strengthen the bond with your children. Using video calls, text messages, or emails to stay in touch, even with a simple "Good morning" message, can help. Setting up a shared online calendar where you and your children can schedule weekly video calls can also maintain a consistent connection.

Establish a regular communication routine, such as a weekly video call or daily message, to keep in touch with your children.

5. Respect Rules

Following court orders demonstrates seriousness and commitment. Adhering to court orders regarding visitation shows respect for legal decisions and can improve your legal standing. Meticulously following all court guidelines demonstrates seriousness and a commitment to resolving the situation fairly.

Keep a diary of visitations and communications with your ex-partner, noting any issues or difficulties encountered, to show your commitment to respecting the rules.

6. Avoid Blame

Remember that your children are victims of the situation, not at fault. Avoid blaming them or making them feel responsible for the conflicts between you and your ex-partner. This can help reduce their guilt and anxiety.

Write a list of positive phrases to use during discussions to avoid placing blame on the children.

7. Be Consistent

Maintaining a consistent and predictable presence in your children's lives is crucial. Continue being the loving and present parent you have always been, despite the difficulties.

Establish a daily routine with regular activities to share with your children, such as reading a bedtime story.

8. Keep Promises

Fulfilling commitments made to your children demonstrates reliability and builds trust. Never break your promises, as this can damage the relationship.

Keep a journal of promises made and ensure to honor all of them, showing your children they can depend on you.

9. Foster Connection

Organizing enjoyable and meaningful activities with your children strengthens your bond. Plan special moments to share together, such as outings or common hobbies.

Plan a special day each month to do something fun with your children, like a trip to the park or a movie night at home.

10. Seek Support

Seek help from professionals experienced in parental alienation. Joining support groups can provide useful advice and a sense of community.

Find a local or online support group for parents in similar situations and regularly attend meetings to share experiences and gain support.

Implementing these practical tips can help create a more serene and supportive environment for children, effectively countering narcissistic parental alienation. In the next section, we will continue with additional practical tips to further strengthen the bond with your children.

Responding Provocations with the BIFF method

Imagine receiving a venomous message from your ex-partner, full of unfounded accusations and criticism. Your first reaction might be to defend yourself or retaliate, but this would only fuel the conflict. This is where the BIFF method (Brief, Informative, Friendly, and Firm) comes in, especially crucial in the context of parental alienation. Parental alienation is a form of psychological abuse, and responding with aggression or manipulation worsens the situation.

Using the BIFF method means keeping responses concise and limited to necessary facts, avoiding personal judgments. It's important to maintain a neutral or friendly tone, avoiding conflict, and being clear and firm in your response. For example, if you receive a message like, "You're never available for your kids and they know it," you could respond: "I picked up the children at 5 PM as agreed. If there are any issues with the timing, we can discuss it civilly."

To avoid falling into provocations, recognize situations that tend to provoke strong emotional reactions and prepare in advance to respond calmly. Practicing mindfulness and meditation techniques can help maintain calm and avoid impulsive reactions. Defining what is acceptable and what is not in communications with the other parent and sticking to these boundaries is equally important.

A parent who applied the BIFF method noticed a reduction in provocations and an improvement in communication with the ex-partner. Brief, informative, friendly, and firm responses made interactions less conflictual and more manageable.

To practice the BIFF method, write brief, informative, friendly, and firm responses to potential provocations you might receive. Simulate different situations with a friend or therapist to strengthen this technique and feel more prepared to handle difficult communications.

By staying calm and not responding to provocations, you can reduce conflicts and improve the environment for yourself and your children, creating a more serene and positive context and effectively countering narcissistic parental alienation.

Chapter 6:
When a Narcissist Turns People Against You

The phenomenon of 'flying monkeys' refers to people whom the narcissist manipulates to do their dirty work, destabilizing and isolating the non-narcissistic parent. 'Flying monkeys' can be friends, family members, colleagues, or even the children themselves, influenced by the narcissist through lies and distortions of reality.

In the context of co-parenting, the narcissist seeks to gain allies among the people close to their ex-spouse by telling them distorted or fabricated stories. For example, a narcissist might start talking to the relatives of the non-narcissistic parent, telling them that the other parent is unstable or unreliable. These tactics aim to isolate the non-narcissistic parent and strengthen the narcissist's control over the situation.

The narcissist is often very skilled at presenting themselves as the victim or the reasonable person while portraying the other parent in a negative light. People who hear these stories, unaware of the narcissist's true nature, can easily fall into the trap and become 'flying monkeys'. This manipulative behavior not only discredits the non-narcissistic parent but also creates an emotionally toxic environment for the children.

For the non-narcissistic parent, seeing friends and family distance themselves can be extremely painful. This isolation can intensify feelings of loss and injustice, making co-parenting even more challenging. Recognizing the phenomenon of 'flying monkeys' is essential for self-defense and for protecting the children. Knowing that the narcissist uses these manipulative tactics helps in preparing and developing effective defense strategies.

Narcissist Tactics Unveiled

narcissists use a range of manipulation and seduction strategies to gain control and influence those close to the non-narcissistic parent. Their ability to present themselves as victims or reasonable people makes these tactics particularly effective and insidious.

One of the main strategies narcissists use is their charm and charisma. They can convince others that they are empathetic and understanding, which makes them very persuasive. For example, they might approach a family member or friend of the non-narcissistic parent and say, "I need to talk to you about something very difficult regarding [parent's name]. I'm sorry to have to tell you this, but I think it's important that you know." In this way, they set the stage to spread lies or exaggerations that paint the other parent in a bad light.

A common example of this dynamic occurs during a divorce. The narcissist, knowing the family and friends of their ex-spouse well, begins to contact them and tell them negative and often false stories. They might say things like, "I worked so hard to save our marriage, but [parent's name] has been so difficult to deal with. Here's what really happened..." These stories are designed to generate sympathy for the narcissist and disdain for the other parent.

The narcissist can also use real events, such as arguments or disagreements, and twist them to their advantage. For instance, if there was a heated argument, the narcissist might tell the children or family members that the non-narcissistic parent reacted excessively or violently, even if it's not true. They may also completely fabricate lies, creating a narrative where the other parent appears as the antagonist.

These tactics not only weaken the support for the non-narcissistic parent but also foster doubt and confusion. The people involved, unaware of the narcissist's true nature, may begin to question their own perceptions and trust the narcissist more and more. This process, known as gaslighting, makes the non-narcissistic parent feel increasingly isolated and insecure.

For the children, these manipulations can be particularly damaging. Growing up in an environment where one parent is constantly denigrated, they can develop a distorted view of reality and relationships. The narcissist may try to convince the children that the other parent doesn't truly love them or doesn't care for them as they should, undermining the parent-child bond.

An exemplary case might be that of a narcissistic father who, during visits with the children, tells them that their mother is not capable of taking proper care of them, exaggerating minor domestic incidents or inventing stories of neglect. This behavior not only creates tension between the children and the other parent but also reinforces the narcissist's control over the family narrative.

Surviving the Narcissist's Smear Campaign

When the narcissist begins to manipulate those around the non-narcissistic parent, the emotional consequences can be devastating. The resulting pain and isolation can deeply affect both the non-narcissistic parent and the children involved.

The immediate effect is a sense of betrayal and confusion. People who once were a source of support and comfort may start to distance themselves, ignore calls, and cancel plans. This behavior can seem inexplicable but is often the result of the manipulative and false stories told by the narcissist. For the non-narcissistic parent, this isolation can intensify feelings of loneliness and despair. The thought of losing contact with close friends and family is painful and can lead to deep sadness and a sense of loss.

A concrete example of this dynamic in the context of co-parenting is a mother who shared custody of her children with her narcissistic ex-husband. The ex-husband, determined to gain total control over the children's lives, started telling the children and relatives that the mother was unstable and incapable of taking care of them. He told the children that their mother often forgot to feed them or left them alone for long periods. These lies, repeated constantly, began to influence the children's perception of their mother. The children, confused and scared, started to prefer staying with their father, believing his stories.

The mother noticed that the children were becoming increasingly distant and reluctant to spend time with her. Even relatives and friends began to treat her coldly, having heard the falsehoods spread by the ex-husband. Feeling isolated and misunderstood, the mother went through a period of deep pain and confusion. She couldn't understand why those close to her were pulling away and what she had done to deserve such treatment. Only when one of her close friends revealed what the ex-husband had been saying did she understand the extent of the manipulation.

The emotional reaction to these situations is complex. The victim may experience a range of emotions, including anger, sadness, frustration, and confusion. There is often a strong sense of injustice, as the non-narcissistic parent has done nothing to deserve this treatment. This can lead to a loss of trust in people and relationships, making it difficult to open up to others again.

For the children, the emotional impact can be just as severe. Growing up in an environment where one parent is constantly denigrated can create confusion and insecurity. Children may begin to doubt their own perceptions and develop a distorted view of relationships. The narcissist may try to convince the children that the other parent doesn't truly love them or doesn't care for them as they should, causing long-term damage to their self-esteem and trust.

To cope with the pain and isolation caused by 'flying monkeys', it is important for the non-narcissistic parent to find ways to process their emotions. This may include talking to a therapist, joining support groups, or finding activities that bring joy and comfort. It is also crucial to try to rebuild damaged relationships by openly communicating with the people involved. Often, those who were alienated can be brought back with time and sincere communication.

Another effective strategy is to educate those around about what is really happening. Without directly accusing the narcissist, the non-narcissistic parent can explain their side of the story and how they feel about the rumors or lies being spread. This approach can help rebuild trust and clarify any misunderstandings.

Effective Strategies to Counter Narcissistic Lies

The first step in effectively responding to 'flying monkeys' is to allow yourself to process the emotions involved. When the narcissist manages to turn people against you, the emotions of pain and anger can be overwhelming. It is crucial to acknowledge these emotions and take the necessary time to address them. Seeking support through therapy can be very helpful at this stage. A therapist can provide a safe space to explore your feelings and develop strategies to handle the situation.

Once you have addressed your emotions, it is important to take a calm and rational approach in dealing with the 'flying monkeys'. One of the most common mistakes is trying to directly defend yourself against the narcissist's accusations. This can often make the situation worse, as the narcissist is skilled at manipulating conversations to their advantage. Instead, try to remain calm and avoid reacting impulsively to provocations.

An effective strategy is to keep communication with the 'flying monkeys' open and honest, without getting into the details of the accusations. You might say something like, "I'm sorry you heard these things. I'm always available for an open and honest conversation if you want to discuss further." This approach demonstrates maturity and openness, without falling into the trap of heated defense.

It is also crucial to build and maintain a solid support network. Surround yourself with trusted people who know your true nature and can offer emotional support. These individuals can help you maintain perspective and avoid feeling isolated. Additionally, having a strong support network can serve as a buffer against the narcissist's manipulations.

When it comes to protecting children from manipulation, the key is open and honest communication. Talk to your children in an age-appropriate way, explaining that sometimes people may say things that are not true. Encourage your children to come to you with any questions or concerns, reassuring them that you are always there to listen and support them.

For example, you might say, "I know you might hear things about me that confuse or worry you. I want you to know you can always talk to me about anything that concerns you. I'm here for you and want you to know how much I love and care about you."

Another useful strategy is to document any manipulative or abusive behavior from the narcissist. Keeping a record of events can be helpful if you need to address legal issues or demonstrate the narcissist's behavior to third parties, such as lawyers or therapists.

Finally, it is important to take care of yourself. Co-parenting with a narcissist can be extremely stressful and exhausting. Make sure to take time for activities that bring you joy and relaxation. This can include hobbies, exercise, meditation, or simply spending time with supportive friends and family.

Consider the case of a mother with a narcissistic ex-husband. The ex-husband, determined to gain total control over the children, starts telling lies to the mother's family and friends, saying that she is unstable and incapable of taking care of the children. During this period, the mother notices that people start to distance themselves and the children seem increasingly confused and distant. Only when one of the family friends reveals what the ex-husband is saying does the mother understand the extent of the manipulation.

In response, the mother decides not to confront the ex-husband directly or defend herself against his accusations. Instead, she calmly talks to the children, explaining that some of the things they hear might not be true and that they can always talk to her about any concerns. At the same time, she works on maintaining her emotional support by talking to friends and family who know her true nature, thus rebuilding trust and security for both herself and her children.

Rebuilding Relationships

The first step in rebuilding relationships is to determine which people are worth recovering. During the period of manipulation, some people may have distanced themselves or believed the narcissist's lies. It is important to reflect on who was truly close and important and which relationships are worth your effort. If someone was easily swayed against you, it might be necessary to consider how solid that bond was in the first place.

Once you have identified who is worth recovering, it is essential to approach these people with grace and sincerity. Instead of defending yourself or attacking the narcissist, try to have open and honest conversations. You can explain that there have been misunderstandings and that you are available to clarify any doubts. For example, you might say, "I know that some things have been said about me that have caused you concern. I'm sorry you had to hear these things, and I would like to clarify the situation with you."

It is important not to get into specific details of the accusations but to stay on a path of reconciliation and openness. This approach can help rebuild trust without fueling further conflict. Additionally, it is important to be patient; some people may need time to overcome the negative influences of the narcissist and regain their trust in you.

Regarding your children, it is crucial to work constantly to strengthen your bond with them. Open communication and reassurance of your love and support are fundamental. The narcissist may attempt to undermine your relationship with your children by telling them that you do not truly love them or that you do not take proper care of them. To counteract this, spend quality time with your children, listen to their concerns, and reassure them of your commitment to them.

Another important aspect of rebuilding relationships is demonstrating your reliability and integrity through actions, not just words. Being consistent in your behavior and keeping promises helps rebuild lost trust. Show your friends, family, and children that they can count on you and that you are there for them consistently and sincerely.

Consider involving a mediator or family therapist if the relationships are particularly damaged. A professional can help facilitate communication and overcome the barriers created by the narcissist's manipulations. Therapy can provide a safe space to express feelings and work together towards reconciliation.

Finally, it is important to accept that some relationships may not be recoverable. Despite all efforts, there will be people who may never come back into your life. Accepting this reality can be painful, but it is essential for moving forward. Focus on the relationships you can save and the new bonds you can build rather than those that have been lost.

Consider the case of a mother who sees her children marginalized in their sports and recreational activities because of the lies told by her narcissistic ex-husband. The ex-husband started spreading falsehoods to other parents and coaches, saying that the mother was negligent and did not truly care about the children. During this period, the mother notices that the children are no longer invited to social events and that the coaches seem to treat her coldly.

To respond, the mother decides not to confront the ex-husband directly or defend herself against his accusations. Instead, she calmly talks to the children, explaining that some of the things they hear might not be true and that they can always talk to her about any concerns. At the same time, she works to maintain her emotional support by talking to friends and family who know her true nature, thus rebuilding trust and security for both herself and her children.

Additionally, the mother decides to speak discreetly and respectfully with the coaches and some parents, trying to clear up any misunderstandings without getting into open conflicts. This approach allows others to see her true nature and recognize the narcissist's manipulations.

Learning from Co-parenting Experiences

Experiencing the manipulations of a narcissist during co-parenting can turn into an opportunity to learn valuable life lessons, fostering significant personal growth and strengthening the ability to prevent future manipulations.

One of the most important lessons is recognizing the warning signs of narcissistic and manipulative behavior. Narcissists are often skilled at hiding their true nature behind a veil of charm and charisma. They may appear to be charming and empathetic individuals, but beneath this facade lie selfish motivations and a desire for control. Learning to recognize these early signs can help you better protect yourself in the future.

Another fundamental lesson is the importance of surrounding yourself with people who know you well and can offer emotional and practical support. These individuals can serve as anchors of stability when you feel overwhelmed by the narcissist's manipulations. Their presence can also help you maintain a balanced perspective and avoid feeling isolated.

Additionally, it is crucial to remember that you are not responsible for the narcissist's behavior. Narcissists are adept at making others feel guilty for their actions and at distorting reality to make it seem like the fault always lies with others. Recognizing that the narcissist's manipulative behavior reflects their insecurities and not your shortcomings can help free you from feelings of guilt and inadequacy.

The lessons learned from these experiences can also help you build healthier and more authentic relationships in the future. Overcoming the challenges of co-parenting with a narcissist can make you stronger, more resilient, and more aware of your capabilities. These experiences, although painful, can lead to a more balanced and fulfilling life.

Chapter 7:
22 Shocking Ways Narcissists Manipulate You

Gaslighting

Have you ever felt confused, doubting your perceptions and your memory? Perhaps, during a discussion, you started to wonder if what you remembered really happened. This is the essence of gaslighting, one of the most insidious manipulation techniques used by narcissists. Imagine telling someone about an incident and hearing, "You're making it all up, it never happened." Or, "You're too sensitive, you always exaggerate." Gradually, you begin to doubt your sanity and trust yourself less and less.

Gaslighting works because it gradually erodes self-confidence. A mother might start doubting her parenting skills because the narcissist insists she is incompetent or distracted. Or a father might be convinced he never said or did something important because the narcissist manipulates memories and distorts reality. This technique is particularly devastating in co-parenting, where clarity and mutual trust are essential for the well-being of the children.

It is crucial to recognize the signs of gaslighting and remember that reality is not just what the narcissist tries to impose. Always remember that your perceptions and feelings are valid.

Playing the Victim

Imagine being involved in a heated discussion, trying to express your concerns, but every time you bring up a critical point, the other person emotionally withdraws, complaining about being attacked and unfairly mistreated. This is the technique of "playing the victim," another weapon in the narcissist's arsenal.

The narcissist presents themselves as the victim in every situation to elicit sympathy and distract from their own faults. In the context of co-parenting, this might mean that any attempt at constructive dialogue is derailed by accusations of injustice and mistreatment. A common example might be: "I can't believe you're treating me this way, after everything I've done for you and the kids." This flips the situation, forcing the other person to defend and justify themselves, instead of addressing the real issues at hand.

The tactic of playing the victim is particularly effective because it exploits the empathy of the other parent, leveraging guilt and responsibility. A co-parent dealing with a narcissist who uses this technique might feel constantly under attack and unable to assert their own viewpoints.

Recognizing this manipulation is the first step to not falling into the trap. It is important to stay calm and focused on the facts, without being drawn into the emotions stirred up by the narcissist's drama.

Triangulation

Imagine being in a private conversation with someone, but suddenly other people are brought into the discussion, creating an atmosphere of tension and competition. This is triangulation, a technique where the narcissist introduces a third person into the dynamic, often to create conflict, jealousy, or rivalry.

Triangulation can manifest in various ways. For example, a narcissist might praise another parent or friend in front of the co-parent, suggesting that this third person is more competent or loving. Or they might relay negative comments supposedly made by others about you, fueling insecurities and suspicions. "You know, your mother thinks you can't handle the kids well," they might say, inserting a destabilizing doubt.

In the context of co-parenting, triangulation can be used to divide and conquer, creating alliances and tensions that undermine cooperation. The children themselves can be manipulated in this process, placed at the center of conflicts and used as pawns to gain advantages or punish the other parent. This not only damages the relationship between the parents but can have devastating effects on the children's emotional well-being.

To defend against triangulation, it is crucial to maintain direct and clear communication, avoiding getting drawn into the narcissist's power games. Establishing clear boundaries and protecting your relationships from external influences can help reduce the impact of this manipulative technique. Recognizing the attempt to create divisions and staying united as parents is essential to preserving a healthy and stable environment for the children.

Love Bombing

At first, it might seem like a fairytale: constant compliments, unexpected gifts, grand gestures, and intense declarations of love. This is love bombing, a manipulation technique where the narcissist overwhelms the other person with extraordinary affection and attention to gain emotional control. At the beginning of a relationship or during a critical moment, these displays might seem genuine and wonderful, but they hide a darker strategy.

Love bombing is designed to create emotional dependency. The victim feels special and uniquely loved, making it difficult to recognize the manipulative intentions behind these gestures. In a co-parenting context, the narcissist might use this technique to regain ground or distract the other parent from real issues. They might suddenly become cooperative and generous, only to disarm the other parent and prepare them for future manipulation.

83

This technique can be particularly confusing because when the narcissist abruptly stops the love bombing, the victim may feel guilty or inadequate, thinking they did something wrong to deserve this loss of affection. This cycle of euphoria and abandonment keeps the victim in a state of uncertainty and vulnerability.

To defend against love bombing, it's essential to recognize that genuine affection doesn't manifest in exaggerated gestures and doesn't have ulterior motives. Maintaining a critical perspective and not getting swept away by the emotions of the moment can help see beyond the facade.

Blameshifting

Have you ever found yourself discussing a problem, only to suddenly have all the blame shifted onto you? This is the technique of blameshifting, where the narcissist diverts attention from their own responsibilities and faults by placing them on others. In co-parenting, this technique can be especially frustrating and demoralizing, as every attempt to resolve an issue turns into a personal attack.

Blameshifting works by shifting the focus from the real issue to a discussion about the other person's culpability. For example, if you try to address inappropriate behavior or a questionable decision made by the narcissist, they might respond with accusations like: "It's your fault the kids act this way; you don't know how to parent them." Or, "If you weren't so stressful, I wouldn't need to act this way." This not only avoids addressing the problem but also makes the victim feel inadequate and responsible for everything that goes wrong.

Blameshifting can create a constant feeling of walking on eggshells. Every mistake or difficulty becomes an opportunity for the narcissist to criticize and undermine the other parent, eroding their confidence and decision-making ability. This creates a toxic environment that harms both the parents and the children.

To counter blameshifting, it's important to stay calm and focused on the facts, not on personal accusations. Remember, everyone is responsible for their own actions, and shifting blame doesn't solve problems but exacerbates them.

Intimidating

Intimidation is a powerful manipulation technique used by narcissists to maintain control and instill fear. This technique can manifest through aggressive behavior, a raised voice, threatening gestures, or even tense silences. The goal is to make the other person feel insecure and afraid to express their opinions or to oppose them.

An example of intimidation might be a parent raising their voice during a discussion about a decision regarding the children, making the other parent feel as if they have no choice but to submit. Or, they might use body language to communicate disapproval and threat, such as clenching their fists or staring intensely at the other parent without speaking. These behaviors create an atmosphere of fear and submission, discouraging any form of dissent.

Intimidation doesn't always require acts of physical violence; often, the implicit threat of emotional or psychological retaliation is enough to control the other person. This can include veiled threats to withdraw the children's affection, create legal problems, or discredit the other parent in the eyes of friends and family. The cumulative effect of these behaviors can be devastating, leading the other person to feel powerless and isolated.

To defend against intimidation, it's crucial to recognize it for what it is and not give in to fear. Maintaining your calm and composure can disarm many of the narcissist's intimidating tactics. Additionally, seeking external support from friends, family, or professionals can strengthen your position and provide strategies for managing intimidating situations. Remember, no one has the right to make you feel insecure or threatened, and maintaining your dignity is essential for resisting this form of manipulation.

Exaggerating

Have you ever noticed how some people tend to dramatize every situation, inflating details until they are almost unrecognizable? This is the technique of exaggeration, a manipulative strategy used by narcissists to distort reality to their advantage. Exaggeration can turn a minor inconvenience into a catastrophe, manipulating others' perceptions and emotions to gain control.

A typical example of exaggeration might be a small oversight, such as not responding to a message right away. The narcissist might react by saying, "You never care about what I say, you always ignore me!" Or, a few minutes' delay might become: "You're always late, you never respect my time!" This magnification of problems creates a sense of urgency and stress, making the other person feel constantly under pressure.

In co-parenting, exaggeration can be particularly damaging. Normal, understandable behavior from the children, like making noise while playing, might be presented as a serious problem: "The kids are out of control, and it's all your fault!" This not only creates tension between the parents but can also make the children feel inadequate and problematic without reason.

To counteract exaggeration, it's important to maintain a balanced perspective and not get swept up in the narcissist's hyperbole. Checking the facts and staying calm can help dismantle the exaggerations. Remember that situations are rarely as dramatic as they are presented and that reality is often much more manageable than the narcissist wants you to believe.

Keeping open and honest communication with your children can also help mitigate the negative effects of this manipulative technique, reassuring them and teaching them to see things in the right perspective.

Labeling

Have you ever had someone unfairly attach negative labels to you or your behavior? This is labeling, a manipulative technique where the narcissist assigns negative labels or stereotypes to discredit and control the other person. This strategy relies on creating reductive and stigmatizing identities, making it difficult for the victim to escape the role they have been assigned.

An example of labeling might be when a narcissistic parent labels the other as "incompetent" or "selfish" whenever they make a different decision. Phrases like "You are always so irresponsible" or "You never think about others" become common, creating a distorted image of the person. This not only damages the other person's reputation but also undermines their self-esteem and confidence.

In a co-parenting dynamic, labeling can lead to serious consequences. For instance, one parent might be labeled as "too lenient" or "too strict," negatively affecting how the children perceive that parent. The children might start internalizing these labels, developing a distorted view of their parents and feeling confused about whom to trust.

To counteract labeling, it's crucial to recognize that labels are tools of manipulation and do not reflect reality. Maintaining open and honest communication with your children can help dispel negative labels and build a relationship based on trust and mutual understanding. Recognizing your own values and capabilities, and not allowing the narcissist's words to define your identity, is essential for maintaining a healthy perspective.

Projection

During a conflict, the narcissist might accuse the other person of faults or behaviors that actually belong to them. This is projection, a manipulation technique where the narcissist attributes their own unacceptable feelings, thoughts, or behaviors to others. By projecting their shortcomings onto others, the narcissist avoids confronting their own flaws and shifts responsibility.

A common example of projection might be a narcissistic parent accusing the other of being emotionally distant or insensitive, when in reality, it is the narcissist who exhibits these traits. Statements like "You're the one who never listens" or "You're always so cold with the kids" are typical and serve to divert attention from their own faults.

In co-parenting, projection can create an atmosphere of confusion and frustration. The parent who is unfairly accused might start to doubt their abilities and perceptions, constantly feeling on the defensive. This undermines their confidence and makes it difficult to address real issues constructively.

To counteract projection, it's important to stay aware of your own emotions and behaviors, distinguishing between what is real and what is the narcissist's manipulation.

Scapegoating

Imagine always being the scapegoat, the person blamed for every problem regardless of the circumstances. This is the technique of scapegoating, a manipulative strategy where the narcissist shifts all blame and responsibility onto another person to avoid confronting their own mistakes and flaws.

The narcissist might use this technique to paint the other parent as the cause of all family problems. Every difficulty, every disagreement, every mistake is attributed to the other parent, creating a narrative where the narcissist is the innocent victim and the other parent is the guilty party. For example, if the children are struggling in school, the narcissist might say: "It's your fault they're not doing well; you're not a good parent."

This constant blame-shifting can erode the other parent's self-esteem and create a toxic family environment. Children, seeing one parent constantly accused and criticized, might develop a distorted perception of reality and internalize these dynamics, believing it's normal to always find someone to blame.

To counteract the scapegoating technique, it's essential to maintain your integrity and remember that everyone has their own responsibilities. Remember, you are not responsible for all the problems, and you deserve to be treated with respect and dignity.

Silent Treatment

In a co-parenting relationship, the silent treatment can be one of the most insidious forms of manipulation. This technique involves using silence and ignoring the other person as a form of punishment and control, leaving them feeling invisible and irrelevant. The narcissist intentionally stops communicating, hoping to emotionally destabilize the other parent and make them feel guilty or anxious.

Imagine trying to discuss an important issue regarding the children, but the other person refuses to respond, turning away or simply ignoring you. This behavior can make the parent on the receiving end of the silence feel powerless and frustrated, unable to resolve issues or make shared decisions. Phrases like "Don't you have anything to say?" or "Why won't you listen to me?" become useless in the face of a wall of silence.

The silent treatment can be devastating, as it isolates the other parent and makes them feel as though their concerns and feelings don't matter. This can lead to a breakdown in effective communication and increased tensions, negatively affecting co-parenting and the children's well-being.

Remember, you deserve to be heard and respected, and the narcissist's imposed silence does not define your value.

Dehumanizing

Remember a time when you felt treated like less than a person, reduced to an object or a function? Dehumanization is one of the cruelest tactics a narcissist can use. This technique involves treating the other parent as if they have no feelings, needs, or intrinsic value, reducing them to something less than human.

Dehumanization can manifest in many ways, from contemptuous words to belittling behaviors. The narcissist might deliberately ignore the other person's feelings, treat them condescendingly, or make them feel insignificant. For example, during a discussion about parenting, they might say things like: "You don't understand anything about this" or "You're incapable of making important decisions." These words not only hurt but aim to destroy the other parent's self-esteem and dignity.

This technique is particularly devastating because it strikes at the core of personal identity and worth. Constantly being belittled can lead to a loss of self-confidence and a sense of worthlessness. Dehumanization not only harms the targeted parent but can also negatively affect the children, who might begin to see one of their parents through the narcissist's distorted lens.

Devaluation

One moment, you are the center of the narcissist's attention, treated with great admiration and respect. Then, suddenly, everything changes. This is devaluation, a technique where the narcissist drastically reduces the other person's worth to maintain control and power. After an initial period of idealization, where the victim is elevated to an almost unreachable level, the phase of devaluation begins, where every flaw is magnified and every mistake becomes a reason for criticism.

Devaluation can be particularly devastating. The narcissist might start criticizing every decision made by the other parent, describing them as incompetent or irresponsible. Phrases like "You never do anything right" or "You're a terrible parent" become common, creating an atmosphere of constant disapproval. This behavior undermines the devalued parent's confidence, making them feel inadequate and insecure.

Devaluation is designed to keep the victim in a state of dependence and insecurity. When a parent is constantly devalued, they may start to doubt their abilities and decisions, making them more susceptible to the narcissist's manipulations. This not only damages the relationship between the parents but can also negatively impact the children, who may absorb and internalize these toxic dynamics.

To defend against devaluation, it is important to recognize your intrinsic worth and not allow the narcissist's words to define your identity. Remember, your value is not determined by the opinion of a narcissist, and you deserve to be treated with respect and dignity.

Displacing

Have you ever noticed how a narcissist can take out their frustrations and anger on you, even when you had nothing to do with what caused them? This is the technique of displacing, where the narcissist directs their negative emotions toward an innocent target to avoid dealing with their own problems.

Displacing can manifest in extremely harmful ways. For example, if the narcissist had a stressful day at work, they might come home and start criticizing the other parent over small things, like how meals are prepared or the management of the children's daily routine. Phrases like "You're useless" or "You can't do anything right" are often used to unload their anger and frustration.

This behavior not only creates a hostile family environment but also makes the targeted parent feel powerless and constantly under pressure. The victim might start walking on eggshells, trying to avoid anything that could trigger another outburst, leading to a life of continuous stress and anxiety.

To counteract displacing, it's crucial to recognize that the narcissist's outbursts are not a reflection of your worth or abilities. Staying calm and not taking these manifestations personally can help reduce their emotional impact.

Emotional Appeals

Emotional appeals are attempts to evoke feelings of guilt, pity, or fear in another person to manipulate them into acting a certain way. These appeals can be particularly effective because they leverage emotions and a sense of responsibility.

Imagine a situation where the narcissist tries to get something from the co-parent by saying, "If you really care about the children, you'll do as I say." Or they might use phrases like, "I feel so lonely without you; you can't do this to me." These emotional appeals are designed to make the other person feel guilty or responsible for the narcissist's well-being, leading them to give in to their demands.

Emotional appeals can create an atmosphere of constant pressure and manipulation. The parent on the receiving end of these appeals may feel compelled to set aside their own needs and desires to satisfy those of the narcissist, even when it's not in the best interest of the children.

To counter emotional appeals, it's important to recognize when emotions are being used as a manipulation tool. Staying firm and remembering what the real priorities are can help resist these attempts at manipulation.

Guilt

Guilt is one of the narcissist's favorite weapons for manipulating and controlling others. Using guilt allows the narcissist to make the other person feel responsible for any discomfort or problem, even when they have done nothing wrong. This creates an emotional dependency where the victim constantly tries to make up for their supposed mistake.

For example, a narcissist might say things like: "If you really cared about the family, you wouldn't do this," or "After everything I've done for you, how can you act this way?" These statements are designed to make the other person feel guilty and compel them to conform to the narcissist's desires. This type of manipulation can be particularly effective because guilt is a powerful emotion that can lead to complete submission.

In co-parenting, the narcissist may use guilt to control important decisions regarding the children. They might make the other parent feel guilty for not spending enough time with the kids or for not following their directives. This creates an environment of constant tension and can undermine the other parent's confidence in their abilities.

Hoovering

Hoovering is a manipulative technique used by the narcissist to suck the other person back into the relationship, much like a vacuum cleaner (hence the term "hoovering"). After a period of distance or breakup, the narcissist may suddenly reappear in the other person's life with messages, calls, or affectionate gestures, pretending to be remorseful or wanting reconciliation.

This technique creates a false sense of hope and manipulates the victim's emotions. Common phrases include "I miss you so much, can we try again?" or "I understand my mistakes, I will change." The narcissist leverages the other person's feelings of nostalgia and desire for stability to regain control.

Hoovering can occur when the narcissist senses they are losing power or influence. For instance, they might suddenly become more involved in the children's activities or display an unusually cooperative attitude, just to draw the other parent back into their manipulative orbit.

Remembering the narcissist's past behavior patterns can help see through their false promises.

Isolation

This method not only allows them to maintain control over the victim but also reduces external support that could help counteract the manipulation. The narcissist might start by criticizing the victim's friends and family, insinuating that they are untrustworthy or a bad influence.

Gradually, the victim finds themselves increasingly isolated, with the narcissist as their only source of support and approval. For example, they might say, "Your friends don't understand you like I do" or "Your family only causes problems." This type of talk erodes external relationships and makes the victim more dependent on the narcissist.

Isolation can mean trying to prevent the other parent from maintaining healthy relationships with friends and family or from participating in social activities. This creates a dynamic where the victim feels trapped and without support, further facilitating the narcissist's control.

It's important to recognize the narcissist's attempts to drive away supportive people. Staying in touch with friends and family, even discreetly, can provide the necessary support to maintain a balanced perspective.

Shame

Shame is a powerful and devastating tool in the hands of a narcissist. They use shame to make the other person feel inferior, forcing them to question their own worth and abilities. This feeling of shame can be paralyzing, causing the victim to withdraw and become easier to control.

The narcissist can exploit every mistake, no matter how small, to make the other parent feel inadequate. Comments like "You're a terrible parent" or "You never know what to do" are sharp weapons aimed at undermining self-esteem and confidence. This leads to a cycle of insecurity and submission, where the victim constantly seeks the narcissist's approval, never feeling good enough.

To combat shame, you have to understand that these comments do not reflect reality. Every parent makes mistakes, and no one should be defined by them. You deserve respect and dignity, regardless of what the narcissist might say.

Stonewalling

Stonewalling can manifest in various ways. The narcissist might simply ignore questions, change the subject, or physically leave the room. This attitude not only frustrates the other parent but also makes them feel isolated and powerless. The lack of communication prevents addressing issues constructively and fuels a cycle of misunderstanding and resentment.

Stonewalling can make managing shared responsibilities extremely difficult. For example, if an important decision needs to be made regarding the children, the narcissist might refuse to discuss it, leaving the other parent to handle the situation alone. This creates an environment of stress and uncertainty, where cooperation becomes almost impossible.

Ghosting

Ghosting is a technique where the narcissist suddenly disappears from the other person's life without any explanation. This behavior creates confusion and distress, leaving the victim wondering what went wrong. The narcissist may cut off all communication, ignore messages and calls, and vanish without a trace.

Imagine trying to contact your co-parent to organize the children's activities or discuss important matters, but receiving no response. This sudden silence can be extremely destabilizing, making the other person feel abandoned and powerless. Ghosting is an extreme form of manipulation, designed to punish and control, leaving the victim in a state of uncertainty and vulnerability.

Ghosting can have particularly severe consequences. The lack of communication makes it impossible to coordinate and collaborate for the children's well-being. The victim is left to manage everything alone, without the narcissist's support, increasing the burden of stress and responsibility.

Invalidation

Invalidation is a manipulative technique to diminish and deny the other person's emotions, thoughts, and experiences. This behavior can manifest in comments like: "You're overreacting," "You're too sensitive," or "It's not that important." The goal is to make the victim feel insecure and doubt their perception of reality.

When your emotions are constantly invalidated, it can be extremely frustrating and disorienting. Imagine expressing a legitimate concern about the children and being met with a comment that minimizes your feelings. This can make you feel unheard and disrespected, leading to a decrease in your self-esteem.

If one parent expresses concerns for the children's well-being and the other parent minimizes or dismisses them, it creates a dynamic where one person's needs and feelings are continually ignored. This can lead to conflicts and misunderstandings, making it difficult to make joint decisions and maintain a healthy environment for the children.

Minimization

Have you ever been told that your concerns are exaggerated or that you're overreacting? This is at the heart of minimization, a technique used by narcissists to downplay the importance of your emotions and experiences. Phrases like "You're making a mountain out of a molehill" or "It's not that big of a deal" make you feel like your concerns don't matter.

Think of a time when you were worried about something concerning your children, and the narcissist responded with indifference, making you doubt the validity of your concerns. This type of reaction not only diminishes your feelings but also undermines your confidence in yourself and your judgment.

Minimization can lead to serious consequences. When one parent tries to discuss important issues and the other constantly downplays them, it creates an environment where one person's needs and feelings are ignored. This makes it difficult to make balanced decisions and can negatively impact the children's well-being.

Your Opinion Matters

Dear reader,

As you reflect on what you've read so far, I want to ask you for a small favor that can make a big difference. Your honest opinion of this book on Amazon can help other parents who are searching for answers. Imagine someone in the midst of a difficult custody battle, feeling isolated and desperate for guidance. Your review can point them towards a resource that could change their lives.

Writing a review is a simple way to give back. It takes just a few minutes, but its impact can be profound. Your opinion can validate the experiences of others, offering them reassurance and practical advice. By sharing what you've found helpful—or even what you think could be improved—you contribute to a community of parents supporting each other through similar challenges.

As an author, I rely on feedback from readers like you to reach more people who might benefit from this book. Your review can help improve the book's visibility, ensuring it reaches those who need it most. Whether your feedback is positive or critical, I appreciate your honest perspective and value every single comment.

Please take a moment to leave your review on Amazon. Your voice can make a real difference in someone else's journey.

Thank you for your support and for being part of this community.

Chapter 8:
10 Real Ways to Set Boundaries With a Narcissist

One of the most damaging effects of interacting with a narcissist is the creation of blurred boundaries. Instead of having a clear distinction between oneself and the other, a confusion arises that prevents recognizing and maintaining one's own identity and needs. This phenomenon, defined as "blurred boundaries," makes it difficult to maintain emotional balance and a clear vision of who you want to be.

The goal of this chapter is to provide a practical and detailed guide on how to establish and maintain healthy boundaries when interacting with narcissistic people. Through ten specific strategies, we will learn to recognize and address narcissistic behaviors, protect our mental health, and strengthen our self-esteem.

These strategies will not only help manage relationships with narcissists better but also contribute to developing greater self-awareness and better emotional self-regulation. Along the way, concrete examples and practical advice will be provided to apply each technique in daily life.

1. Understanding the Psychology of the Narcissist

To establish effective boundaries with a narcissist, the first step is to understand the psychology behind their behavior. Narcissists often appear as extremely self-confident, imposing individuals who desire to dominate every situation. However, behind this facade lies deep insecurity and an intense fear of inadequacy.

In an attempt to protect themselves from their fears, these individuals develop a strong need for control. They cannot allow the people around them to be too independent or distinct, as this would threaten their sense of well-being and power. It is crucial to recognize that their domineering behavior and need to dominate stem from inner fragility and a constant state of fear.

When interacting with a narcissist, it is helpful to keep in mind that behind their mask of arrogance and strength lies a frightened child. This awareness can radically change our approach to them, allowing us not to take them too personally and not to be overwhelmed by their manipulations.

Understanding these dynamics helps us maintain a clear perspective and avoid the trap of wanting to please or appease the narcissist at all costs. Instead, we can focus on maintaining our boundaries and protecting our emotional well-being. Knowing who the narcissist really is and what motivates their behavior is the fundamental first step in interacting with them in a healthier and more conscious way.

2. Knowing Your Limits

Once you understand the psychology of the narcissist, the next step to establishing effective boundaries is knowing your own limits. When dealing with someone who has strong narcissistic tendencies, it's essential to know when and how long to interact with them. This means having a clear definition of what you can and cannot tolerate.

Often, we find ourselves in situations where we have to interact with the narcissist in various contexts, such as work, family, or friendships. In these cases, it's easy to feel overwhelmed and want to avoid the person altogether. However, this feeling of exhaustion and frustration may stem from not having set clear limits for ourselves.

Defining your limits involves deciding how much time and under what circumstances you are willing to spend around the narcissist.

For example, you might need to limit interactions to once a month or only for specific events. It's important to be honest with yourself about your capacity to handle the stress and discomfort these interactions may cause.

Setting these limits doesn't mean being rude or completely avoiding the person; rather, it means protecting your emotional well-being. It's an act of self-care and respect for your own needs. If you know that a certain amount of time with the narcissist is the most you can tolerate without compromising your peace of mind, you must stick to that limit without feeling guilty.

This self-discipline will help you maintain a position of strength and balance in your interactions. Knowing when to say "enough" and taking the necessary time to recharge your energies is crucial for managing relationships with narcissists. This way, you can avoid being dragged into toxic dynamics that damage your self-esteem and mental health.

3. Listening to Your Emotions

A crucial part of establishing boundaries with a narcissist is listening to your own emotions. When interacting with a narcissist, it is normal to experience a range of negative emotions such as anger, frustration, or fear. These emotions should not be ignored, as they provide crucial signals on how to handle the situation.

For instance, if you feel anger towards a narcissist who is being overbearing and oppressive, that anger is trying to tell you something. Anger is your way of signaling that this person is going against you and that your boundaries are being threatened. It is a signal of self-preservation, a warning that indicates the need to adopt assertive behaviors. Being assertive means expressing your needs and establishing clear boundaries in a respectful and firm manner.

Similarly, if you feel defensive around a narcissist, this emotion indicates fear. Defensiveness is a signal telling you that you perceive the person as a threat or as someone who is not trustworthy. It is important to listen to this feeling and make decisions that protect your emotional safety. If a narcissist constantly makes you feel threatened or insecure, you may need to limit the time you spend with them or even avoid contact altogether.

Listening to your emotions also involves recognizing when it is time to step away from a situation that is becoming too stressful. If you notice that your anxiety levels increase every time you have to interact with the narcissist, it may be necessary to take a break and reflect on how you can better manage these interactions in the future. Ignoring or suppressing these emotions can lead to an accumulation of stress and frustration, making it even more difficult to maintain healthy boundaries.

4. Ignoring Overbearing Behavior

Narcissists often try to impose their opinions and control situations by telling you what to do and how to behave. In these moments, it's essential to remember that you have the right not to engage in these dynamics.

When a narcissist forcefully expresses their opinions or tries to dictate how you should act, you can choose not to engage in the discussion. It can be helpful to simply ignore their attempts at control and stand your ground. For example, if the narcissist insists on a particular way of doing things, you can calmly and confidently respond that while that is their opinion, you have a different perspective and will follow your own path.

Ignoring overbearing behavior does not mean being passive or submissive, but rather consciously choosing not to get involved in unnecessary arguments or manipulations. This way, you can maintain your autonomy and continue doing what you believe is right without having to constantly justify your choices.

There are times when the narcissist may try to provoke you or elicit a reaction through aggressive or insistent behavior. In these situations, staying calm and not reacting can be a very effective strategy. Showing that their words and actions have no power over you can disarm the narcissist and reduce their desire to control you.

5. Saying No Without Guilt

Narcissists often try to involve you in situations that benefit them but may not be in the best interest of you or your children. It is crucial to recognize that you have the right to refuse and to do what is best for you and your family.

For example, the narcissist might insist that the children participate in events or activities that you know are stressful or inappropriate for them. They might want to change visitation schedules at the last minute without considering the children's needs or your family plans. Or, they might try to impose their own parenting style, disregarding your preferences and the need for consistency for the children.

In these situations, it is important to be clear and direct in communicating your disagreement. You can simply say, "I don't think that's the best thing for the children," or "I prefer to stick to our current schedule." There is no need to go into lengthy explanations or justifications. Your decisions are based on the well-being of your children, and you have the right to uphold them.

Learning to say no is a form of self-care and respect for yourself and your children. It is a way to establish healthy boundaries and protect your family's emotional well-being. You may feel guilty initially, especially if you are used to avoiding conflicts with the narcissist. However, it is essential to remember that saying no does not make you a bad or selfish person; it makes you a parent who is aware of your children's needs and ready to take care of them.

The narcissist might not react well to your refusal and might try to make you feel guilty or manipulate you into changing your mind. Maintain your position calmly and firmly. The more you practice saying no, the more natural it will become, and the less guilt you will feel.

Saying no without guilt is a crucial step to keeping your boundaries intact and avoiding situations that are not in your children's best interest. This approach will help you strengthen your self-esteem and protect your family's emotional balance.

6. Maintaining Privacy in Relationships

A fundamental aspect of establishing effective boundaries with a narcissist is not sharing personal information with them. This might seem sad, especially if you're a relational person who likes to share joys, disappointments, and significant moments with others. However, with a narcissist, this openness can be used against you.

Narcissists tend to gather personal information to find ways to gain an advantage over you. Any detail you share can be weaponized and reused in the future to manipulate you or to consolidate their power. Therefore, it is better to maintain a certain emotional distance and not reveal deep aspects of your life.

For example, if you tell the narcissist about a difficulty you are going through, they might use it to undermine your self-esteem or to attack you at a moment of vulnerability. Or, if you share a joy or success, they might belittle it or use it as a starting point for competition. To protect yourself from these risks, it is essential to limit the information you share and keep conversations on superficial and neutral topics.

Maintaining privacy in relationships with a narcissist is a self-defense strategy. While it might seem cold or distant, it is a necessary step to protect your emotional well-being. By doing so, you reduce the opportunities for the narcissist to manipulate you or create conflicts based on your personal vulnerabilities.

Remember that the less the narcissist knows about you, the better off you are. Keep your boundaries well-defined and do not let your private life become a playground for narcissistic manipulations. This will help you preserve your peace of mind and manage interactions with the narcissist in a safer and more controlled manner.

7. Not Participating in the Criticism of Others

Narcissists often speak poorly of others to seem superior and manipulate your perception of the people around you. They try to make you doubt others and push you to share their negative opinions. To protect your boundaries, it is crucial not to engage in this criticism.

When a narcissist starts speaking badly about others, such as friends, colleagues, or family members, avoid getting drawn into it. They might badmouth "Jane," "Susie," or "Tom," belittling their abilities or character. This behavior is the narcissist's way of asserting that their viewpoint is correct and they try to involve you to legitimize their opinions.

In these situations, it is important to maintain your stance and not get dragged into the criticism. You can respond with phrases like, "I prefer to accept people for who they are," or "That's their business, I'm not interested in discussing it." By doing so, you avoid fueling the narcissist's critical attitude and keep your boundaries clear and intact.

Avoiding participation in the criticism doesn't mean you have to actively defend the people being talked about but rather maintain a neutral position and refuse to engage in negative behavior. This helps protect your integrity and prevents the narcissist from using your words against you in the future.

By maintaining this position, you show the narcissist that you are not willing to participate in their manipulative dynamics. This not only protects you but also sends a clear message to the narcissist: you cannot be used as a tool for their negative purposes.

8. Not Defending Yourself from Insults

When interacting with a narcissist, it is almost inevitable that they will throw insults or severe criticism at you at some point. Phrases like "You are the dumbest person I've ever met" or "You don't know what you're talking about" can become common. These verbal attacks often say more about the narcissist's issues than about you.

It is important to remember that constantly defending yourself against these insults can be exhausting and often ineffective. Repeatedly explaining yourself or your decisions to a narcissist can lead to further criticism and attacks, perpetuating a toxic cycle. After clarifying your position once, it is better to avoid prolonged arguments.

When the narcissist insults you, try not to defend yourself. Instead, you can respond calmly and firmly, making it clear that their words do not affect you. For example, you might say, "I don't care about your opinion on this," or simply not respond at all. Showing that their insults have no power over you can disarm them and reduce their motivation to continue.

Another effective approach is to let the narcissist know that their impressions of you are irrelevant. For example, you might say, "Your words don't change what I think about myself." Narcissists hate feeling irrelevant, so this type of response can be particularly effective.

Remember, you don't have to justify yourself to someone who uses criticism as a tool of manipulation. By staying calm and not reacting to insults, you protect your self-esteem and show that you are not influenced by the narcissist's attempts to belittle you.

Not defending yourself from the narcissist's insults is a powerful strategy for maintaining your boundaries and preserving your emotional health. By showing that their words do not affect you, you strengthen your position and reduce the control the narcissist can have over you.

9. Being Kind but Not Trying to Change the Narcissist

When interacting with a narcissist, it's important to remember that kindness should not be used as a means to try to change their behavior. While it may feel natural to be kind and understanding, this approach can often backfire with narcissists.

Narcissists tend to interpret kindness as a sign of weakness or as an opportunity to manipulate you further. If you try to use kindness to reason with them or to get them to see things from your perspective, they are likely to see this as an advantage for themselves, strengthening their position of power.

For example, you might think that being particularly understanding and accommodating will lead the narcissist to change their attitude or show more respect. However, most of the time, what happens is that the narcissist uses this kindness to continue to pull the strings and keep you entangled in their web of manipulations.

Being kind is certainly preferable to being rude or aggressive, but it's important not to expect that your kindness will change the narcissist. Your kindness should be a personal choice and not a strategy to try to alter the behavior of someone who has no intention of changing.

A good approach is to maintain a kind and respectful attitude without trying to use this kindness to influence the narcissist's behavior. You can be polite in your interactions, but you also need to be firm and clear about your boundaries. For example, you might say, "I respect your opinion, but this is my decision," without trying to convince them or expecting them to accept your view.

By maintaining kindness as a personal value rather than a tool for change, you protect your integrity and ensure that your kindness is not exploited. This allows you to interact with the narcissist without falling into the traps of their manipulations and without sacrificing your dignity.

10.   Investing in Healthy Relationships

A crucial aspect of maintaining boundaries with a narcissist is investing time and energy in healthy relationships. Often, narcissists try to become the center of your life, wanting everything to revolve around them. This can lead to progressive isolation, as the narcissist does not want you to have positive experiences and external support that can strengthen your self-esteem and emotional balance.

To counter this, it is essential to cultivate relationships with people who appreciate you for who you are and who genuinely support you. Surround yourself with friends, family, and colleagues who respect your boundaries and value your individuality. These positive relationships provide essential emotional support and help you maintain a balanced perspective on your life.

For example, spending time with friends who listen to and understand you can help you recharge and feel less alone. Participating in social activities and groups with common interests can offer opportunities to create new connections and strengthen existing ones. In this way, you build a support network that sustains and protects you from the narcissist's toxic dynamics.

Investing in healthy relationships is not just about seeking emotional support but also about sharing moments of joy and satisfaction with people who value you. These positive experiences remind you that you are capable of building relationships based on mutual respect and trust.

Maintaining healthy relationships also helps strengthen your boundaries with the narcissist. When you know you have people you can rely on, you are less likely to tolerate manipulative behavior and more capable of defending your rights and well-being. Remember that the healthy people in your life are a constant reminder that you deserve respect and kindness.

Chapter 9:
15 Key Lesson You MUST Know

1. Lower Your Expectations

After the divorce, it's unlikely that the narcissist's behavior will improve; in fact, it often gets worse. Their need to feel like they're winning and to exert control becomes even more pronounced. Expecting the narcissist to adhere to legal agreements or keep promises can lead to disappointment. For instance, if the court has ordered a certain amount of child support or specific visitation schedules, the narcissist may try to sabotage these agreements to assert their power.

Mentally preparing for these possibilities helps maintain control over the situation. Planning for the narcissist not to do what they're supposed to allows you to anticipate problems and reduce stress. Adopting a pragmatic and realistic approach is essential. Knowing that your ex-partner won't take the "high road" and will try to manipulate situations to their advantage is a reality you must accept.

So, the key is to lower your expectations, plan for the worst, and hope for the best. This mindset not only provides emotional protection but also helps you stay focused on what's most important: the well-being of your children and your own peace of mind.

2. Don't Fall for Attention-Seeking Tactics

One of the typical behaviors of narcissists is doing whatever it takes to draw attention, especially in co-parenting contexts. It's essential not to fall for their emotional manipulation attempts. The narcissist might try to change plans at the last minute, requesting schedule changes or demanding to have the kids for the holidays, just to create chaos and maintain control.

These requests are often strategies to test your limits and see how much they can manipulate you. For instance, the narcissist might suddenly claim they want to spend the holidays with the kids, despite previous agreements, just to ruin your plans. They know that holidays are special times and use this fact to destabilize you and reassert their presence.

The key is to stay calm and always have a plan B. Anticipating these behaviors and preparing to respond firmly, without getting emotionally involved, is crucial. Setting clear boundaries and refusing to deviate from established agreements without a valid reason helps maintain control of the situation.

Additionally, having an alternative plan for holidays or any other important events reduces stress and allows you to better manage the inevitable manipulations. Remember, the narcissist's goal is to attract attention and create disorder; don't let this affect your and your children's well-being.

3. Communicate Only About the Children

It's crucial to limit communication strictly to topics related to the children. Discussing personal matters or past issues can only give the narcissist more opportunities for manipulation and conflict. Focusing solely on the needs and well-being of the children is essential for maintaining as peaceful an environment as possible.

An effective strategy is to establish clear boundaries: all communications should be about the children and preferably conducted via text or email. This not only creates a written record that can be useful in case of legal disputes but also reduces the chances of misunderstandings or verbal manipulations. For example, any changes to visitation schedules, school issues, or medical needs of the children should be addressed in writing.

Moreover, it's important not to respond to provocations or communications that fall outside the scope of child-related topics. If the narcissist tries to discuss personal issues, the best approach is to ignore those messages and only respond to ones relevant to co-parenting. This helps keep the focus on what truly matters and avoids unnecessary conflicts.

Lastly, keeping communication brief, clear, and focused helps reduce stress and better manage the co-parenting relationship. Remember, the goal is to protect your children's well-being and maintain a functional and respectful relationship, despite the challenges posed by the narcissistic behavior of your ex-partner.

4. Respond Only to Reasonable Communications

In a co-parenting relationship with a narcissist, it's essential to respond only to reasonable communications. This means addressing messages only if they are respectful and relevant to the needs of the children. Establishing this rule helps maintain clear and functional communication, reducing the risk of emotional manipulation and unnecessary conflict.

To ensure this, it's helpful to set specific criteria for what constitutes a reasonable communication. For instance, the message should directly pertain to the children, be expressed in a civil and respectful tone, and contain clear and factual requests or information. If the message doesn't meet these criteria, there's no need to respond.

Another important aspect is the response time. Allowing yourself at least 24 hours to respond to communications, except in cases of emergency, gives you time to reflect calmly and formulate a considered response. This time interval reduces the likelihood of impulsive reactions and provides the opportunity to consult with a lawyer or counselor if needed.

Maintaining this discipline in responding only to reasonable communications helps create a more stable and predictable environment for the children. Additionally, it limits the narcissist's power to disrupt your emotional peace and allows you to keep the focus on what truly matters: the well-being and serenity of your children.

5. Take Time to Respond

Taking time to respond to communications is a crucial strategy. Establishing a 24-hour interval before replying, except in emergencies, helps avoid impulsive reactions and allows for a thoughtful and considered response.

This waiting period offers several benefits. First, it helps calm any intense emotions triggered by the narcissist's message, such as anger or frustration. Taking a pause allows for emotional distance from the situation, enabling a more objective evaluation of the communication's content. Additionally, it provides the opportunity to consult with a lawyer or counselor if necessary, ensuring that the response is appropriate and protective of your interests and those of your children.

Writing the response in a separate document, like a notepad, before sending it is another useful method. This allows you to review and edit the text calmly, ensuring that the tone remains respectful and professional, and avoids any expressions of frustration or anger.

Ultimately, this practice helps establish a more predictable and controlled communication rhythm. Reducing impulsive responses and maintaining composure towards the narcissist helps better manage the co-parenting relationship, preserving your own peace of mind and protecting the well-being of your children.

6. Recognize Projections

A typical behavior of narcissists is projection, which involves attributing their own thoughts, feelings, or behaviors to others. Recognizing this mechanism is crucial for managing co-parenting with a narcissist. Understanding that what the narcissist accuses you of doing or feeling is often a reflection of their own actions or emotions can help you avoid falling into their emotional traps.

For example, a narcissist might say, "You don't care about the kids," when, in reality, they are the ones who are not genuinely involved in the children's lives. This statement serves to distract from their own shortcomings and put you on the defensive. Knowing that projection is one of their tools, you can interpret these accusations as indications of what is actually happening in their mind.

When you recognize a projection, it's important not to react emotionally. Stay calm and respond only to the relevant facts concerning the children. This approach helps you remain centered and prevents the narcissist's emotional manipulations from disrupting your peace of mind.

Additionally, documenting these projections can be useful in case of legal disputes. Keeping a record of communications and unfounded accusations helps build a clearer picture of the narcissist's manipulative behavior, providing concrete evidence if needed. Recognizing and managing projections is a key skill for navigating the complex dynamics of co-parenting with a narcissist.

7. Be the Best Parent Possible

When co-parenting with a narcissist, it's essential to be a positive role model for your children. Narcissists often use children for their own ends without validating their feelings. Therefore, it's crucial to show love, understanding, and support.

Listen to your children and validate their feelings, creating a safe and loving environment. For example, talk with them about their day and their emotions, responding with empathy and attention. Maintain calm and rationality even in difficult situations, avoiding negative talk about the other parent in front of the children.

Being the best parent possible promotes your children's healthy growth and counteracts the negative influence of the narcissistic parent's behavior. By consistently showing love and understanding, you help your children grow up in a balanced and positive environment.

8. Always Accept the Children

When the narcissist asks to change custody schedules or have more free time, always agreeing to take the children is a key strategy. While it may seem inconvenient or demanding, accepting these requests without swapping turns is crucial for documenting the reality of the situation.

Always taking the children whenever the narcissist asks for a schedule change demonstrates your commitment and dedication to your kids. This behavior not only protects their well-being but also highlights the narcissist's lack of interest in quality time with the children. By documenting each request and schedule change, you can build a strong case showing the narcissist's failure to adhere to custody agreements.

For example, if your ex-partner asks to change the visitation weekend at the last minute, agree to take the children but insist on keeping the original schedule for future visits. This approach shows your flexibility and dedication to the children while highlighting the other parent's unreliability.

This strategy is particularly useful in legal contexts, where documentation can clearly demonstrate who is the more stable and present parent. By always accepting the children, you protect their well-being and better prepare yourself for any future legal disputes.

9. Validate Your Children

Narcissists tend to ignore or belittle children's emotions, causing confusion and insecurity. As a parent, it's crucial to be the one who listens and acknowledges their feelings, providing constant emotional support.

Take the time to talk with your children about their emotions and concerns. Ask them how they feel and what they think, showing genuine interest in their responses. For example, if a child expresses sadness or frustration about something that happened with the other parent, acknowledge their feelings by saying, "I understand that you feel sad; it's normal to feel that way in this situation."

Also, avoid minimizing or denying their emotions. Phrases like "You shouldn't feel that way" can make children feel unheard and invalidated. Instead, give them the space to express themselves freely and reassure them that their feelings are important and legitimate.

Being the parent who validates and emotionally supports the children helps build their self-esteem and resilience. This approach counteracts the negative influence of the narcissist and creates a safe and loving environment where the children can grow up feeling understood and valued. Consistently validating their emotions strengthens your bond with your children and promotes their psychological well-being.

10. Avoid Speaking Negatively About the Ex

It's crucial to avoid speaking negatively about the other parent in front of the children. Although it can be challenging, especially in high-conflict situations, it's important to remember that children need to feel safe and loved by both parents.

Speaking negatively about the ex can create confusion and emotional stress for children, who may feel pressured to take sides. This can harm their emotional development and their perception of family relationships. Additionally, children might feel guilty or responsible for the conflict, which can negatively affect their self-esteem.

Instead of criticizing the ex-partner, focus on how you can support your children. Answer their questions neutrally and reassuringly, providing only the necessary information appropriate for their age. For example, if they ask why their parents are no longer together, a simple response like "Mom and Dad decided to live separately, but we both love you very much" is sufficient.

Showing respect for the other parent, even when it's difficult, teaches children the importance of mutual respect and healthy conflict resolution. This approach helps create a stable and positive environment where children can feel loved and supported by both parents.

11. Stay Calm and Rational

Narcissists tend to create conflict and tension, trying to provoke emotional reactions. It's essential not to get drawn into these dynamics and to maintain a balanced demeanor.

An effective strategy is to mentally prepare for provocations. Knowing in advance that the narcissist will try to manipulate you can help you stay centered. For instance, during face-to-face interactions, take deep breaths and remind yourself not to respond immediately to provocative or negative comments.

Staying rational also means avoiding discussions about personal or past issues. Focus solely on relevant facts about co-parenting and the children's needs. This approach not only reduces the chances of conflict but also sets a good example of mature and responsible behavior for your children.

Remaining calm and rational not only protects your mental health but also provides your children with a model of healthy and constructive behavior. Teaching them how to handle conflicts calmly and respectfully is one of the best gifts you can give them, especially in a complex co-parenting situation.

12. Document Everything

Documenting every interaction and incident is essential when co-parenting with a narcissist. Keeping a detailed record of all communications, requests for schedule changes, and any problematic behavior can make a significant difference in case of legal disputes.

For example, every time the narcissist asks for a schedule change or violates an agreement, note the date, time, and specific details of the incident. Save all relevant emails, text messages, and notes from conversations. This provides a paper trail that can be useful in demonstrating a pattern of unreliable or manipulative behavior.

Additionally, documenting everything helps you stay calm and rational. Knowing that you have an accurate record of interactions can reduce stress and anxiety, allowing you to respond more thoughtfully and strategically. It can also deter the narcissist from attempting to manipulate you, knowing that their actions are being monitored.

Keep these records in a safe place, such as a password-protected file on your computer or a cloud storage service. Ensure that only you and, if necessary, your lawyer have access to this information.

Documenting everything is a protective measure for both you and your children, ensuring that you can handle any legal issues with solid and well-organized evidence.

13. Seek Outside Support

Seeking outside support is crucial when co-parenting with a narcissist. Handling the challenges of this dynamic can be extremely stressful and draining, so having someone to talk to who can offer practical advice and emotional support is essential.

One effective way to get support is to see a therapist or counselor who specializes in relationships with narcissists. These professionals can help you develop strategies to manage manipulation and maintain your mental health. They can provide tools to stay calm, improve communication, and protect yourself emotionally.

Participating in support groups, whether online or in person, can also be very helpful. Sharing your experiences with others who are facing similar situations can provide a sense of community and understanding. Knowing that you are not alone in this can make a big difference to your emotional well-being.

Trusted friends and family can also offer valuable support. Don't hesitate to talk to them about your difficulties and ask for their help. Having a strong support network can help you stay strong and resilient, giving you the energy and courage needed to face the challenges of co-parenting with a narcissist.

Lastly, consider seeking legal resources to protect your rights and those of your children. A family law attorney can provide you with advice and assistance in navigating the legal complexities of the situation. Seeking outside support is not a sign of weakness, but a smart strategy to handle a difficult situation and ensure the well-being of you and your children.

14. Focus on Your Well-Being and Personal Growth

Taking care of yourself is essential when co-parenting with a narcissist. Finding moments to relax and engage in activities that bring joy and tranquility, like reading a book or taking a walk, helps reduce stress and recharge your energy.

Setting personal goals and working towards them can boost your self-esteem and provide a sense of accomplishment. Whether it's advancing your career or learning a new skill, focusing on these milestones offers a positive direction.

Surrounding yourself with positive and supportive people, such as friends and family, is equally important for overall well-being. Additionally, seeking professional help if needed can provide emotional support and strategies for managing stress.

Maintaining your well-being and focusing on personal growth is crucial during co-parenting with a narcissist because it allows you to face challenges with greater strength and resilience. This not only makes you better equipped to handle manipulations and conflicts but also enables you to be a better parent, providing your children with a stable and loving environment.

Chapter 10:
7 Steps to Create a Co-Parenting Plan

A co-parenting plan is a written agreement that outlines how separated or divorced parents will manage responsibilities and make decisions regarding their children. This plan includes details about physical and legal custody, visitation, communication, medical and educational decisions.

Creating a co-parenting plan is crucial when dealing with a narcissistic ex-partner. Narcissists tend to manipulate and create conflicts, making co-parenting extremely difficult. A well-defined plan reduces opportunities for abuse and manipulation by establishing clear and predictable rules.

A well-structured plan helps maintain stability for the children and minimizes conflicts between parents. This is especially important with a narcissist, as clarity and consistency are essential to protect the children's emotional well-being and prevent them from being drawn into toxic power dynamics.

Additionally, a well-drafted co-parenting plan can serve as a legal tool to enforce agreements and document any violations, providing an extra layer of protection and security.

Step 1: Physical Custody and Scheduling Time with Children

Physical custody determines with which parent the children will live and how time will be divided between the two parents. In a co-parenting situation with a narcissist, it is crucial to define every detail to avoid manipulation and conflicts. A clear plan includes specific days and times for visits, as well as procedures for exchanges.

It's important to establish a well-structured schedule that considers the children's needs and offers them stability. For instance, planning exchanges in a neutral location can reduce tensions. Additionally, you should consider the children's specific needs, such as extracurricular activities, school holidays, and family traditions, ensuring both parents have quality time with the children.

The plan should also include how to handle changes or emergencies, such as sudden illnesses or unforeseen commitments. Defining these situations in advance helps prevent disagreements and ensures smoother communication. With a narcissistic ex-partner, maintaining flexibility is essential but always within the limits set by the plan.

Step 2: Legal Custody and Important Decisions

Legal custody involves the right to make significant decisions in the children's lives, such as those related to education, health, and overall well-being. In a co-parenting situation with a narcissist, it is crucial to clearly outline who has the right to make decisions and how these decisions will be made.

A co-parenting plan should specify which decisions require mutual consent and which can be made individually. For example, decisions regarding major medical treatments or school changes should be made jointly to ensure both parties are involved and informed. This helps prevent one parent from making unilateral decisions that might not be in the best interest of the children.

The plan should include a dispute resolution process to handle disagreements that may arise. This can involve mediation or the involvement of a family counselor. Defining these mechanisms in advance helps manage conflicts more effectively and reduces the risk of further manipulation.

Finally, it's important to establish how communication regarding legal decisions will be handled. Using tools like email or online platforms can ensure all communications are traceable and transparent, thus reducing the chances of misunderstandings or manipulations.

Step 3: Exchanges and Communication Between Parents

Child exchanges between parents can be delicate, especially with a narcissistic ex-partner. A co-parenting plan should specify how and where exchanges will occur to reduce conflicts. Neutral locations like schools or community centers can minimize direct contact and prevent clashes.

Defining specific exchange times and using a shared calendar helps adhere to agreements and reduces manipulation. Communication between parents must be clear, concise, and documented. Using tools like email or co-parenting apps ensures traceability and limits misunderstandings. Avoid undocumented verbal communications.

The plan should include guidelines for sharing important information about the children, such as school or medical updates, ensuring both parents are informed and involved. This approach reduces conflict opportunities and promotes effective collaboration for the children's well-being.

Step 4: Medical Care and Child Health

The plan should include provisions for medical emergencies and regular doctor visits. It's essential to establish who is responsible for medical decisions and how they will be made.

Both parents need to be informed about important medical issues, including vaccinations, specialist treatments, and long-term care plans. The plan should specify who attends medical appointments and how associated costs are shared, reducing conflict and manipulation. For instance, parents might agree that both should be notified in advance and have the right to attend appointments, or routine decisions can be handled by one parent with the other's consent.

Lastly, having a method to resolve disagreements about medical decisions can help address conflicts quickly, ensuring the child's needs are always prioritized.

Step 5: Education and Extracurricular Activities

The plan should specify who has the authority to make significant educational decisions, such as school enrollment, changing schools, or selecting special programs.

Both parents should be informed and involved in educational decisions, including regular communication about academic progress, teacher meetings, and participation in school events. Using a shared calendar can help keep track of all school commitments and extracurricular activities, ensuring no appointments are missed.

For extracurricular activities, the plan should outline how programs will be chosen and how costs will be divided. It is useful to set guidelines on how many activities each child can participate in simultaneously and how schedules will be managed to avoid overlaps and conflicts.

Finally, the plan should include a method for resolving any disagreements about educational matters and extracurricular activities. This can involve mediation or the involvement of a school counselor, ensuring that all decisions are made in the child's best interest.

Step 6: Childcare and Parenting Guidelines

It's essential to clearly establish how daily childcare tasks, such as meal preparation, personal hygiene, and bedtime routines, will be managed. Specifying these responsibilities helps ensure consistency and stability in the children's lives, reducing potential conflicts between parents.

The plan should include guidelines on discipline, recreational activities, and technology use. Agreeing on these aspects in advance can prevent disagreements and ensure that children receive consistent messages from both parents. For example, setting common rules for electronic device use and study times can help maintain a balanced routine.

Additionally, it's important to determine how to handle everyday decisions that don't require both parents' consent, such as organizing playdates, choosing clothing, and managing minor health issues. Clearly defining these responsibilities can reduce opportunities for manipulation by a narcissistic parent.

Step 7: Financial Aspects and Child Support

It's important to clearly establish how children's expenses will be managed, including maintenance, medical, educational, and extracurricular costs. Well-defined financial agreements reduce conflicts and ensure children's needs are always met.

The plan should detail how expenses will be divided and managed. This might include defining each parent's percentage share of costs or using a joint account for children's expenses. Documenting expenses, such as with receipts or an online platform, is also helpful.

Additionally, the plan should outline how to handle unforeseen expenses, like medical emergencies or special educational needs. Defining these situations in advance can prevent conflicts and ensure timely fulfillment of children's needs.

Finally, it's important to include a method for reviewing and updating financial agreements as circumstances change, such as increasing educational expenses or medical needs. This ensures the plan remains adequate and sustainable over time.

Step 8: Conflict Resolution and Plan Review

It's important to establish clear methods for managing disputes, such as mediation or involving a family counselor. This approach can prevent escalation and ensure decisions are made in the children's best interest.

The plan should include regular meetings between parents to discuss necessary adjustments, considering the evolving needs of the children. Regular review allows the plan to adapt to new circumstances, like changes in school activities or medical needs.

Having a mechanism to document and report violations of the plan can provide a solid basis for legal interventions, ensuring both parents adhere to agreements and prioritize the children's well-being.

Chapter 11:
How to Handle Narcissists' False Accusations

False accusations are the narcissist's weapon of choice. Imagine being constantly under an invisible attack, where every move is interpreted in the worst possible way. This is what many people experience in a co-parenting relationship with a narcissist. Have you ever wondered why these accusations are so common?

The narcissist uses these tactics to maintain control and destabilize the other parent. These accusations can range from absurd to gravely defamatory: accusations of abuse, neglect, infidelity, and wasting money. Nothing is too extreme if it serves to manipulate others' opinions and maintain power.

Take, for example, a common situation where a parent, after the relationship ends, is overwhelmed by unfounded accusations. Every action, from daily expenses to childcare, is twisted and presented as proof of incompetence. They find themselves having to defend their reputation while trying to maintain stability for their children.

This behavior is not just a matter of spite. False accusations are a calculated strategy to provoke an emotional reaction. The narcissist seeks to leverage the other person's fears and insecurities, hoping to make them appear unstable and weaken their position. Understanding this dynamic is the first step in neutralizing their power.

Responding Without Reacting

When faced with false accusations from a narcissist, the first thing to remember is not to react impulsively. The narcissist aims to provoke an emotional reaction to fuel conflict and gain satisfaction. Responding without reacting means staying calm and composed, avoiding the emotional trap.

Imagine receiving a baseless accusation through a legal document or written communication, such as an email. The temptation to respond immediately can be strong, but it's essential to pause and reflect. A concrete example might be receiving an accusation that questions your parenting abilities. Instead of reacting with anger or frustration, you can take a measured approach, responding calmly and professionally.

For instance, you can acknowledge the message and state that the accusations will be addressed appropriately in due course. This approach shows self-control and prevents the narcissist from using your emotional reaction against you. Remember, the narcissist wants to make you appear unstable; maintaining calm and responding with composure is the best way to counter this tactic.

Responding without reacting requires practice and discipline, but each time you manage to stay calm and respond thoughtfully, you reduce the power the narcissist has over you. It's a crucial step in maintaining control of the situation and protecting your emotional integrity.

Document Everything

One of the most effective strategies for dealing with a narcissist's false accusations is detailed and accurate documentation. Narcissists often contradict themselves and ignore court orders, and this lack of consistency can become a weapon in your favor.

Documenting everything means recording every interaction, every communication, and every relevant behavior. This includes emails, messages, phone conversations, and in-person meetings. For example, if you receive an email where the narcissist accuses you of not paying child support, keep that communication and note the details. Similarly, if the narcissist contradicts themselves in different communications, highlight these inconsistencies.

It's important to keep this information organized and easily accessible. You can use a digital filing system or a simple notebook, as long as it's well-structured. Real-time documentation is crucial; trying to recall past events can be difficult and inaccurate. For instance, immediately note any abusive or irregular behavior.

This approach not only helps you stay calm and composed, but also provides concrete evidence that can be presented in court. Judges despise liars and narcissists who ignore court orders, and your documentation can clearly demonstrate this behavior.

Documenting everything is an essential step to protect yourself from the manipulations and unfounded accusations of the narcissist, allowing you to build a strong position based on solid evidence.

Avoiding Getting Pulled into Fights

When a narcissist falsely accuses you, they often try to drag you into a fight. They want to provoke an emotional reaction, hoping you'll lose your temper and react impulsively. This behavior fuels their need for control and supports their narrative of you as an unstable person. Therefore, it's crucial not to get pulled into their fights.

To handle these situations, an effective approach is to adopt a detached attitude. Imagine observing the situation as an outsider. This allows you to see the narcissist's provocations for what they are: manipulation attempts. For example, if the narcissist starts a dispute by accusing you of not taking proper care of the children, instead of reacting with anger, respond calmly and professionally, focusing on the facts.

In an interview, an experienced judge suggested viewing provocations as an external observer, recognizing that the narcissist is deeply unhappy. This approach helps you avoid getting dragged into conflict and maintain your emotional stability.

Additionally, anticipate the narcissist's behavior as predictable. Expect them to act according to their patterns and be prepared not to react. This means not being surprised when they act manipulatively, but rather being ready to respond with calm and composure.

Avoiding getting pulled into fights is crucial for maintaining control of the situation and protecting yourself from the narcissist's manipulations. Every time you manage to stay calm and not react, you reduce their power over you and strengthen your position.

Resisting Guilt Trips

Narcissists often try to make you feel guilty as a way to manipulate and control you. This tactic can manifest through comments designed to insinuate that you are not a good parent or partner. For example, they might say things like, "I thought you were a better parent," or "You don't really care about your family." These manipulative attempts are meant to make you doubt yourself and keep you in a state of anxiety and uncertainty.

It's essential to become impervious to these guilt trips, as if you were coated in Teflon. When the narcissist tries to make you feel guilty, it's important to remember that these accusations are often projections of their insecurities and do not reflect reality. For instance, during a confrontation, the narcissist might try to guilt-trip you over decisions or actions you've taken, even when you know you've acted in the best interest of your children.

Every time you hear that internal critical voice, ask yourself if it's really your voice or the narcissist's. Often, after years of manipulation, it's easy to confuse the two.

Another strategy is to set clear boundaries and keep interactions with the narcissist brief and unemotional. For example, if the narcissist tries to start a discussion to make you feel guilty, respond calmly and firmly without getting emotionally involved. This not only protects you but also prevents the narcissist from using your emotions against you. Resisting guilt trips and maintaining your integrity reduces the narcissist's power over you.

Using a Single Method of Communication

When dealing with a narcissist, limiting communication channels is crucial to avoid being overwhelmed by manipulation. Using a single, traceable method of communication, such as email, is essential. This allows you to maintain a clear and organized record of interactions, which can be useful in legal situations.

The narcissist will try to push you to use more informal or harder-to-track communication methods, like phone calls or in-person meetings. It's important to resist this pressure and insist on the agreed-upon channel. For example, email allows you to document every exchange, preventing the narcissist from distorting conversations.

If you have children, using a specific co-parenting app might be helpful. In any case, ensure that the chosen method is monitorable and secure. It might be beneficial to obtain a court order mandating the use of a single communication method. This makes it easier to prove any violations by the narcissist and provides an additional layer of protection.

Limiting interactions to a single method of communication helps you maintain control, reduce stress, and create a safer environment for managing the relationship with the narcissist.

Avoiding Being Alone with the Narcissist

Avoiding being alone with the narcissist is a crucial strategy to protect yourself from their manipulations. During child exchanges or other necessary interactions, the narcissist may try to distort reality, creating false conversations or agreements that never took place.

For example, after a child exchange, you might receive a message from the narcissist claiming that you agreed to switch weekends, an agreement that never actually happened. These fabrications are difficult to dispute without witnesses.

To prevent these issues, it is advisable to arrange child exchanges in public places or in the presence of other people. For instance, conducting exchanges in front of the school, with the help of a third party, or in well-frequented areas can reduce the risk of false accusations.

Additionally, limiting communications to traceable means such as email or specific co-parenting apps provides an additional layer of protection. This allows you to keep an accurate record of all interactions, which can be useful in legal disputes.

These precautions not only reduce the likelihood of being falsely accused but also help maintain your peace of mind and manage interactions with the narcissist in a safer and more organized manner.

Chapter 12:
7 Strategies to Destroy a Narcissist in Court

1. Don't React to Provocations in Court

Facing a narcissist in court can be extremely challenging, especially when they try to provoke you with outrageous claims. It is crucial to remain calm and not react to these provocations. Even the calmest people can find it difficult to hold back when false or absurd statements are made about them. However, maintaining control over your emotions is essential. Showing the judge and jury that you can manage your emotional reactions is vital to avoid appearing like the narcissist. Conversely, you don't want to seem completely emotionless: finding a balance is key.

Lawyers often train victims to keep a composed face throughout the proceedings, identifying the right moments to express the sadness from the pain endured. The narcissist's reactions, especially when pushed to the edge, can reveal their true nature. Lawyers aim to elicit narcissistic rage to demonstrate to the jury that the victim is truly the harmed party. Staying calm and accepting criticism with composure can be a winning strategy to expose a narcissist in court.

2. Asking Suggestive Questions

An effective strategy to expose a narcissist in court is to ask suggestive questions. Narcissists don't want anyone to think they are anything less than perfect. Lawyers exploit this trait by asking targeted questions that highlight their flaws. For example, they might ask, "Is the narcissistic spouse capable of showing empathy towards the children?" or "Is it true you haven't spoken to your children in three months?" These types of questions are designed to put the narcissist under pressure and provoke anger.

In divorce cases, lawyers know that these questions can trigger a strong emotional reaction. They want questions that contradict the narcissist's initial statements or other witness testimonies. The goal is to demonstrate to the judge and jury that narcissism was the root cause of the issues and that the victim is truly the victim. Additionally, if children are involved, lawyers will try to show how narcissistic behavior has negatively impacted their lives.

Here are some examples of suggestive questions that can be used in court:

- "Is it true that you told your children that the family problems were their mother's/father's fault?"

- "Have you ever tried to isolate your partner from their friends or family?"

- "Can you explain why you sent these threatening messages to your partner?"

- "Why did you prevent your partner from accessing the family finances?"

- "Have you ever denied your partner permission to work or study?"

- "How do you justify frequently changing the household rules without consulting anyone?"

Lawyers look for evidence of aggressive behavior. They know the jury wants to see concrete proof to determine if they are indeed dealing with a narcissist. Even though it can be challenging to prove, the right questions during depositions can ignite the necessary spark to reveal the narcissist's true nature.

3. Document Everything

One of the most effective tactics to defeat a narcissist in court is to meticulously document every interaction and behavior. Lawyers stress the importance of collecting evidence in the form of text messages, emails, and letters written by the narcissist to the victim. Any evidence of verbal or physical abuse must be carefully preserved. Additionally, it's crucial to gather clues of manipulation or episodes of gaslighting.

Sometimes the narcissist will attempt to contact the victim outside of court. It's essential to document every interaction, including recording phone calls. Narcissists often don't imagine that their calls might be recorded, and they might threaten or verbally abuse the victim without realizing that these actions could backfire in court.

Lawyers look for any negative communication that can put the narcissist in an unfavorable light. Third-party testimonies are equally important: at least one person has likely witnessed or heard the abuse. Witness statements can be crucial to the case. Documenting contacts with the narcissist's friends or family is also critical, as they might be involved in attempts to manipulate or intimidate the victim.

Here are some practical documentation tips:

- Save all communications such as text messages, emails, letters, and voice notes securely.

- Record phone calls if it's legal in your state to capture threatening or abusive behavior from the narcissist.

- Keep a detailed diary with dates, times, and details of every episode of abuse or manipulation.

- Gather testimonies from friends, family, or colleagues who can write statements about what they have seen or heard.

- Preserve physical evidence such as photographs of injuries, screenshots of conversations, and other tangible items that can support the accusations.

Finally, it's important to gather every possible piece of evidence that shows the narcissist in a position of guilt. Meticulous documentation can provide the court with a clear and undeniable picture of the narcissist's true nature, significantly increasing the victim's chances of success.

4. Involving Eyewitnesses

A crucial tactic to defeat a narcissist in court is to involve friends and family who have witnessed the abuse. Lawyers understand the importance of having external witnesses who can confirm the victim's accusations. These witnesses may have overheard threatening phone calls, witnessed episodes of gaslighting, or seen physical signs of abuse on the victim's body.

The testimonies of people who have directly observed the narcissist's behavior can make a significant difference in court. If the witnesses also have documentation, such as photos of injuries or text messages between the narcissist and the victim, this evidence can further strengthen the case. It is essential that witnesses are willing to testify in court and provide detailed accounts of what they have seen or heard.

Sometimes narcissists are unaware that other people know about their abuse. Involving these witnesses can catch the narcissist off guard, making them feel vulnerable. This tactic can also demonstrate to the jury that the narcissist has tried to maintain a facade of perfection while hiding their abusive behavior.

Here are some practical tips for involving eyewitnesses:

- Identify witnesses among friends, family, or colleagues who might have seen or heard something relevant. It is important to consider who might have had direct or indirect access to situations of abuse or manipulation.

- Collect written statements from the witnesses, asking them to describe in detail what they have observed, including specific dates, places, and contexts. These statements can provide a clear and coherent picture of the events.

- Ask witnesses for additional documentation, such as photos of injuries, text messages, or emails that can support their testimony. This type of evidence can be crucial to corroborate the abuse allegations.

- Prepare the witnesses for the trial, ensuring they are ready to speak in court. Explaining the importance of their testimony and what to expect during the process can help them feel more confident and comfortable.

- Work closely with the lawyers, providing all the information about the witnesses so they can prepare effective questions and present the evidence in the best possible way. Good communication between the victim, witnesses, and lawyers is essential to building a strong case.

The presence of eyewitnesses can be decisive in revealing the true nature of the narcissist and achieving justice. Involving external witnesses strengthens the victim's credibility and offers an objective perspective on the abuse suffered.

5. Using the Silent Treatment

One of the most effective tactics to destabilize a narcissist in court is the silent treatment. Narcissists love being the center of attention and hate being ignored, diminished, or made to feel unloved. Using the silent treatment in court can be a powerful weapon, as it's a technique narcissists often use against their victims but hate when it's turned against them.

The silent treatment involves deliberately ignoring the narcissist, avoiding responses to their provocations, and leaving them uncertain about your thoughts and feelings. This behavior can cause significant discomfort for the narcissist, leading them to lose control and exhibit their narcissistic rage.

In court, the silent treatment can be particularly effective. When the narcissist doesn't get the desired reaction from the victim, they may become increasingly frustrated and eventually reveal their true aggressive and manipulative nature in front of the judge and jury. Ignoring the narcissist and not falling for their provocations can show that the victim is in control of the situation and is no longer willing to endure their abuse.

Here are some practical tips for using the silent treatment:

- Avoid any emotional reaction to the narcissist's provocations, maintaining a calm and composed demeanor.

- Do not respond to the narcissist's accusations or insinuations, letting them speak without showing any sign of being upset.

- Focus on your own statements and testimonies, ignoring the narcissist's interruptions and manipulations.

- Work with your lawyer to prepare to maintain strategic silence throughout the process.

The silent treatment can deprive the narcissist of control and demonstrate their inability to handle a lack of attention. When used correctly, this tactic can be crucial in exposing the narcissist in court and achieving justice for the victim.

6. Showing You're No Longer a Victim of Bullying

Demonstrating in court that you are no longer a victim of bullying is a crucial tactic to defeat a narcissist. Narcissists hate feeling inferior and cannot stand those who do not submit to them. During the trial, showing the judge and jury that you have overcome fear and are no longer under the narcissist's control can destabilize them.

When you exhibit confidence and determination, the narcissist may lose their composure. Seeing that the victim is no longer willing to tolerate their abuse can provoke the narcissist into reacting aggressively, revealing their true nature. This behavior can help the judge and jury understand who the real culprit is.

Here are some practical tips for showing that you are no longer a victim of bullying:

- Maintain a confident posture and assertive body language throughout the process. Your physical presence can convey a strong message of inner strength.

- Answer questions clearly and calmly, without showing signs of fear or hesitation. Prepare with your lawyer to respond effectively and confidently.

- Show that you have taken steps to improve your life, such as seeking psychological support or joining support groups. This can demonstrate to the judge and jury that you are proactive in your healing journey.

- Avoid falling into the narcissist's provocations, maintaining control of your emotions even in the face of accusations or insults.

Demonstrating to the court that you are no longer a victim of bullying and have regained control of your life can be crucial in achieving justice. Your strength and determination can destabilize the narcissist and reveal their true nature.

7. Consulting a Therapist Before the Trial

Consulting a therapist before the trial can be extremely helpful in defeating a narcissist in court. By talking to a therapist, the victim can receive professional support and emotionally prepare to face the narcissist. The therapist can provide accurate and impartial statements about what is happening in the victim's domestic life, highlighting signs of narcissistic abuse.

The therapist can testify in court, offering an expert assessment of the victim's mental and emotional state and confirming whether they exhibit symptoms of prolonged abuse. This testimony can be crucial as it comes from a qualified and impartial professional. The narcissist may not expect the victim to have sought professional help, and this can further destabilize them.

Here are some practical tips for consulting a therapist:

- Find a therapist who specializes in narcissistic abuse and relational trauma, someone who can thoroughly understand the dynamics of narcissistic abuse.

- Keep a detailed record of therapy sessions, including dates and topics discussed, which can be presented as evidence in court.

- Ask the therapist to testify in court and prepare them with the help of your lawyer.

- Use the therapist's evaluations and statements in your testimony to strengthen your case.

Consulting a therapist not only helps the victim heal and gain emotional strength but also provides solid evidence and professional testimony that can be decisive in defeating a narcissist in court. This move can demonstrate to the jury the depth of the abuse suffered and the victim's determination to regain control of their life.

Managing Custody Order Violations

Violations of custody orders are a common and significant issue that can have serious legal and personal repercussions. When a parent does not comply with a custody order, the other parent has several legal options. Willful and intentional violation of a court order is considered "contempt," a criminal action that can result in fines, jail time, or both. Contempt is a punitive measure that can be directly requested by the affected parent, regardless of law enforcement involvement.

Contempt represents a deliberate and knowing disobedience of a court order. This violation can be reported and prosecuted through a specific legal process, which may include severe penalties like fines or imprisonment. To initiate a contempt action, the parent who has experienced the violation must formally file a request with the court, documenting the other parent's noncompliance. For example, if a father fails to deliver the child to the mother as stipulated in the custody order, the mother can turn to the court to report the incident and request appropriate sanctions.

Beyond contempt, violating a custody order can also provide grounds for requesting a modification of the order itself. Disobedience of the existing custody order can be seen as a material change in circumstances, justifying a review of the order. When considering a modification, the court evaluates whether the noncompliant parent's behavior is against the child's best interest. For instance, if a father repeatedly fails to adhere to the custody schedule, this behavior can be interpreted as an abuse of the authority granted by the court and may lead to a revision of the custody arrangements.

A request for modification of the custody order can be submitted together with the contempt request or separately. In either case, the goal is to protect the child's welfare and ensure that custody provisions are followed. The court may decide to limit or revoke the custodial rights of the noncompliant parent, reassign custody to the other parent, or take other measures it deems appropriate.

A practical example illustrates this situation well: if a mother is supposed to receive her child at 6:00 PM on Sunday and the father, aware of this obligation, does not show up, the court may view this violation as evidence that the father is abusing his custodial authority. This behavior not only violates the court order but also demonstrates that the father is not acting in the child's best interest, thereby compromising his role as the custodial parent.

Contempt and custody order modification are essential legal tools for addressing violations of custody orders. They aim to ensure that parents comply with court decisions and that the child's welfare remains the central focus of custody-related decisions. Each case is unique and requires careful evaluation by an experienced attorney, but knowing these options can help parents protect their rights and those of their children.

Immediate Remedies and Legal Fee Reimbursement

When a parent blatantly violates a custody order, immediate actions can be taken to resolve the situation without having to wait for standard court procedures. In cases of serious violations, the affected parent does not necessarily have to wait to obtain the necessary relief. There are procedures in place that allow for emergency orders or shortened waiting times.

An emergency order request can be made when the custody order violation poses an immediate risk to the child or when waiting for a court decision could cause significant harm. In these cases, the parent can request an "order shortening time," which allows for a modification of the custody order in a much shorter timeframe, often within days or weeks. This tool is particularly useful in emergency situations caused by the noncompliant parent.

For example, if a father arbitrarily decides not to return the child to the mother during her custody time, the mother can go to court to obtain a temporary order granting her full physical custody until the court has a chance to review and modify the custody order permanently. This allows for a swift resolution to standoff situations and protects the child's welfare without the lengthy wait of a standard hearing.

Another important aspect is the reimbursement of legal fees. When a parent is forced to go to court to enforce a custody order due to the other parent's misconduct, they can request reimbursement for the legal expenses incurred. Generally, the court may decide that the noncompliant parent should cover the legal costs of the parent who had to take action to enforce the order. This principle is based on the idea that one parent's wrongful behavior should not financially burden the other, who was compelled to undertake legal action to protect their and the child's rights.

For instance, if a father repeatedly fails to adhere to custody arrangements, forcing the mother to seek court enforcement, the court can order the father to pay the mother's legal fees. This measure serves not only to compensate the aggrieved parent but also to deter the noncompliant parent from continuing to violate custody orders.

In conclusion, there are several immediate legal remedies available to address custody order violations and ensure the protection of the child's and the parent's rights. Emergency requests and legal fee reimbursement are effective tools to handle urgent situations and ensure that a parent's misconduct does not go unpunished. Each case should be individually assessed by an experienced attorney, but knowing these options can help parents navigate these difficult situations with greater confidence and protection.

Chapter 13:
How to Protect Your Child

Understanding Childhood Trauma and Narcissistic Abuse

Understanding childhood trauma and narcissistic abuse is crucial for protecting your children from a narcissistic ex-partner. Often, the narcissistic behaviors of a parent can create a highly dysfunctional and harmful environment for children, profoundly affecting their emotional and psychological development.

Childhood trauma refers to extremely stressful or traumatic experiences that a child is unable to fully process or understand. These traumas can include physical, emotional, or sexual abuse, neglect, or exposure to violent situations. Early life experiences, particularly in the first seven years, are critical for the development of an individual's personality and relational abilities. It is during this period that the foundation for the future is laid, and a safe, stable family environment is essential for healthy development.

Narcissistic abuse, in particular, represents an insidious form of emotional abuse. A parent with narcissistic traits or narcissistic personality disorder tends to use their children to meet their own emotional needs, manipulating and controlling them through alternating affection and criticism. This creates an unpredictable and confusing environment for the child, which can lead to severe long-term emotional and psychological damage.

Narcissism can manifest in various ways. In Freudian psychoanalysis, a "healthy" narcissism during childhood is recognized, where young children go through a phase of believing they are the center of the universe. Under normal conditions, this childhood narcissism is outgrown over time. However, in the presence of trauma or abuse, this narcissism can evolve into problematic narcissistic traits or even into a full-blown narcissistic personality disorder.

The dynamics of narcissistic abuse are complex and often involve cycles of abusive behavior alternating with moments of apparent affection and remorse. This cycle, known as "trauma bonding," reinforces the narcissist's power and makes it difficult for the victim to recognize and escape the manipulation. The narcissist manipulates the victim's emotions, creating an emotional dependency that can be extremely challenging to break.

An example of how this manifests is in narcissistic parents who use their children as tools to fulfill their own needs. They alternate between severe criticism and excessive praise, creating an unstable and insecure environment. This type of behavior can undermine the child's self-esteem and negatively impact their emotional and psychological development.

Understanding these dynamics is essential for protecting children from further harm. Recognizing the signs of narcissistic abuse and intervening promptly can help mitigate the negative effects and promote a healthier, more stable environment for the children. In the next chapter, we will delve into the nature of narcissism, differentiating between narcissistic traits and narcissistic personality disorder, and their respective manifestations and implications.

Is Narcissism a Trait or a Disorder ?

Narcissism can be both a personality trait and a full-blown mental disorder. Understanding this distinction is crucial for protecting your children and taking appropriate action.

Narcissistic traits are characteristics that can appear to varying degrees in everyone. These include a sense of grandiosity, an excessive need for admiration, and a certain lack of empathy. In controlled measures, these traits can even be considered normal and functional. However, when narcissistic traits persist into adulthood and start interfering with daily functioning and interpersonal relationships, they can evolve into narcissistic personality disorder.

Narcissistic personality disorder is characterized by a grandiose sense of self-importance, fantasies of unlimited success, a constant need for admiration, a sense of entitlement, interpersonal exploitation, a lack of empathy, envy of others, and arrogant or haughty behaviors. People with this disorder not only exhibit a wide range of narcissistic behaviors but also use them manipulatively and destructively in their relationships.

Pathological narcissism often stems from traumatic experiences during childhood, which prevent the child from developing a stable and secure sense of self. This disorder generally develops in response to highly traumatic childhood circumstances. These experiences lead to the formation of a "false self" that protects the individual from emotional vulnerabilities. This false self becomes a rigid armor that prevents authentic emotions from emerging.

A practical example of this dynamic is the case of celebrities who, according to some studies, may develop a specific type of narcissism following a rapid rise to fame. Although this type of narcissism is less common than the full-blown disorder, it demonstrates how intense external circumstances can profoundly influence personality development.

It is also important to note that narcissistic personality disorder is considered relatively rare. For it to develop, unique and highly traumatic circumstances during childhood are necessary. A person with this disorder has a psychological structure in which authentic emotions are buried under a facade of grandiosity and manipulation. This makes it extremely difficult for those affected to change their behavior, even with therapeutic intervention.

It is essential to recognize that narcissism exists on a spectrum. Not everyone who exhibits narcissistic traits suffers from a full-blown disorder. However, once a person surpasses a certain level on this spectrum, change becomes extremely unlikely. Relationships with individuals suffering from this disorder can be particularly harmful and challenging to manage, especially for partners and children.

How To Prevent Your Child From Becoming A Narcissist

Narcissism can develop during childhood due to a complex set of factors, including trauma and emotional abuse. Understanding these factors is crucial for recognizing early signs and taking appropriate action to protect children.

The first seven years of life are critical for an individual's personality development. During this period, children form the foundations of their sense of self and their relational abilities. A safe and stable family environment is essential for healthy emotional development. However, when a child is exposed to trauma or emotional abuse, their development can be severely compromised.

One of the main factors contributing to the development of narcissism is the experience of trauma or emotional abuse. These traumas can stem from various sources, including emotionally abusive parents, neglect, or exposure to violence. When a child is constantly criticized, ignored, or manipulated, they develop defense mechanisms to protect themselves from emotional pain. One of these mechanisms is the construction of a "false self," a facade the child uses to hide their vulnerabilities.

This false self becomes a rigid armor that prevents authentic emotions from emerging. The child learns to suppress their feelings and present a grandiose image of themselves to gain approval and admiration from others. This process of constructing the false self is at the core of pathological narcissism.

Another factor that contributes to the development of narcissism is a dysfunctional family dynamic. In a narcissistic family, parents may alternate between excessive praise and severe criticism, creating an unpredictable and insecure environment for the child. This type of behavior can confuse the child and undermine their self-esteem. For example, a narcissistic parent might lavish praise on the child for their successes but harshly criticize them for their failures. This creates a situation where the child learns to value themselves based on others' approval rather than developing intrinsic self-esteem.

Another common dynamic in narcissistic families is the division of roles among the children, often labeled as the "golden child" and the "scapegoat." The golden child is idealized and can do little wrong in the eyes of the narcissistic parent, while the scapegoat is constantly criticized and blamed for everything that goes wrong. This division creates tension among siblings and can lead to severe emotional and psychological issues.

Children exposed to these environments learn to develop narcissistic traits as a survival mechanism. The golden child may grow up with an exaggerated sense of importance and a constant need for admiration, while the scapegoat may develop feelings of inferiority and insecurity. Both roles prevent children from developing a balanced and healthy sense of self.

Another element to consider is the influence of behavioral modeling. Children learn by observing and imitating the behaviors of adults. If a parent exhibits narcissistic traits, it is likely that the child will mimic these behaviors. For example, a child may learn to be manipulative, arrogant, or overly concerned with their external image by observing the narcissistic parent's behavior.

Finally, it is important to note that not all children exposed to trauma or dysfunctional family dynamics necessarily develop a narcissistic personality disorder. There are many protective factors that can intervene, such as the support of other significant adults, early therapeutic interventions, and the child's individual resilience.

Understanding how narcissism can develop during childhood is essential for prevention and effective intervention. Recognizing early signs and providing a safe and supportive environment can help mitigate the damage and promote healthy development.

To prevent the development of narcissism in children, it's essential to adopt strategies that promote healthy emotional and social growth. Here are some effective tactics:

1. Teach Appreciation and Gratitude:

Teaching children appreciation and gratitude can be part of daily routines. For example, during meals, encourage them to express gratitude for the food and for those who prepared it. You can create a family ritual where every evening, before bed, each family member shares three things they are grateful for that day. This not only helps children develop a grateful attitude but also helps them reflect on the positive aspects of their lives, fostering a more optimistic and fulfilling worldview.

Practical example: If a child receives a gift, encourage them to write a thank-you note. This simple gesture can teach a lot about the value of appreciation and the importance of acknowledging others' efforts.

2. Accept and Correct Mistakes:

Accepting and correcting mistakes is essential for personal growth. When a child makes a mistake, instead of punishing them severely, discuss what went wrong and what they could do differently next time. This approach promotes a positive attitude towards learning and reduces the fear of failure.

Practical example: If a child accidentally breaks an object, use the situation as an opportunity to discuss what happened and to find a solution together. For instance, they might save their allowance to help replace it, teaching them responsibility and managing consequences.

3. Allow Facing Consequences:

Allowing children to face the consequences of their actions is crucial for their development. For example, if a child forgets to do their homework, let them experience the natural consequence of receiving a poor grade. This teaches responsibility and the importance of organization and commitment.

Practical example: If a child refuses to wear a coat on a cold day, let them feel the cold for a short period (always ensuring their safety). This practical experience will teach them the importance of listening to parental advice without unnecessary insistence.

4. Offer Sincere Praise:

Offering sincere and merit-based praise is critical for developing self-esteem. Instead of giving generic praise, be specific about what they did well. This type of feedback is more meaningful and helps children understand their strengths.

Practical example: If a child completes a drawing, instead of just saying "Nice!", you might say "I really like how you used colors to create the sunset." This specific praise shows the child that you noticed their effort and specific talent.

5. Spend Quality Time:

Spending quality time with children is crucial for their sense of security and value. This time should be dedicated to activities the child enjoys and that strengthen the emotional bond. For example, reading together every evening not only promotes language development but also creates a ritual of intimacy and connection.

Practical example: Plan weekly activities like cooking a new recipe together, taking a walk in the park, or playing a board game. These moments don't have to be elaborate or expensive; the important thing is that the child feels they have your undivided attention and interest.

6.   Show Respect for Others' Feelings:

Teaching children to respect others' feelings helps them develop empathy and healthy interpersonal relationships. Encourage them to consider how their actions affect others. For example, if a child says something hurtful to a friend, discuss how that friend might feel and suggest ways to make amends.

Practical example: Role-playing different scenarios can be very effective. You can pretend to be someone who has been hurt by their words or actions, and then guide them in understanding and expressing empathy.

7.   Do Not Tolerate Aggression:

Addressing aggressive behavior immediately helps children understand that such actions are unacceptable. If a child hits a sibling or a pet, calmly explain why the behavior is wrong and what the appropriate response should be.

Practical example: Establish clear rules and consequences for aggressive behavior. If a child hits, for instance, they might lose a privilege, such as screen time. Reinforce positive behavior by praising them when they handle conflicts peacefully.

8.   Encourage Humility:

Encouraging humility involves helping children recognize their strengths while understanding they are part of a larger community. Highlighting the importance of teamwork and cooperation can balance their self-view.

Practical example: Involve children in group activities where cooperation is key, such as team sports or group projects. Praise their efforts in working well with others, not just their individual achievements.

9. Promote Face-to-Face Interactions:

Limiting screen time in favor of face-to-face interactions fosters authenticity and social skills. Encourage activities that involve direct communication, such as playing board games or participating in group outings.

Practical example: Organize regular family game nights where everyone is encouraged to interact without the distraction of screens. This not only improves communication skills but also strengthens family bonds.

10. Create Genuine Connections:

Building genuine connections with children involves being present and engaged in their lives. Show interest in their activities, listen to their concerns, and provide emotional support.

Practical example: Set aside time each day to talk about their day, listen to their stories, and discuss their feelings. This consistent attention and support help children feel valued and understood.

Early Signs of Narcissism in a Child & Advice

Recognizing the signs of narcissism in children is crucial for timely intervention and promoting healthy emotional development. Although children under 18 cannot be diagnosed with narcissistic personality disorder, they can still exhibit narcissistic traits that, if not addressed, can evolve into more serious issues in adulthood.

- *Excessive Concern with Appearance:* One warning sign is an excessive concern with appearance. Children developing narcissistic traits may spend a lot of time and attention on their image, showing an exaggerated interest in clothes, hair, and accessories. This behavior often reflects a desire to gain approval and admiration from others, often at the expense of other aspects of their lives, such as schoolwork or genuine friendships.

- *Sense of Superiority and Arrogance:* Another indicator is a sense of superiority and arrogance. Narcissistic children may act as if they are better than others, showing little respect for peers and adults. This attitude can manifest as a lack of empathy and manipulative behaviors, where the child constantly seeks to control and be the center of attention.

- *Constant Need for Admiration:* Children with narcissistic traits often constantly seek admiration and approval from others. They may become highly competitive and have difficulty accepting criticism or failure. This incessant need for recognition can lead them to exaggerate their achievements and downplay those of others, creating a toxic social environment.

- *Manipulation and Control:* Manipulation is another hallmark. Narcissistic children may use various methods to manipulate friends, teachers, and family members to get what they want. These behaviors include lying, deceit, and attempts to induce guilt in others. Manipulation becomes a means to maintain control and gain personal benefits.

- *Difficulty in Social Relationships:* Social relationships can be particularly problematic for children with narcissistic traits. They may struggle to maintain long-term friendships due to their egocentric and manipulative behavior. Often, other children may distance themselves, recognizing the toxic nature of their interactions.

- *Extreme Reactions to Criticism:* Finally, a significant sign is extreme reactions to criticism. Narcissistic children may respond with anger, frustration, or emotional withdrawal when receiving negative feedback. This inability to handle criticism reflects an underlying emotional fragility, masked by a facade of confidence and grandiosity.

Timely intervention is crucial to prevent these traits from solidifying. Here are some strategies to help children develop a more balanced and healthy sense of self:

- Promote Empathy: Teach children the importance of understanding and respecting others' feelings. Activities such as volunteering and open discussions about emotions can help develop empathy.

- Value Effort, Not Results: Praise effort and dedication rather than results. This helps children understand that personal worth is not solely dependent on external successes.

- Set Rules and Limits: Provide a clear structure with consistent rules and consequences. Children need to know that manipulative and disrespectful behaviors will not be tolerated.

- Model Positive Behaviors: Be an example of respect, honesty, and compassion. Children learn by observing adults, so it is important to demonstrate the behaviors you want them to emulate.

- Offer Emotional Support: Create an environment where children feel safe expressing their feelings and concerns. Listening attentively and providing emotional support can help strengthen their inner security.

Recognizing and addressing signs of narcissism in children is essential for promoting healthy emotional development. Timely intervention with targeted strategies can help prevent these traits from becoming entrenched and leading to more serious problems in the future.

The Scapegoat vs The Golden Child

Within narcissistic families, a particular dynamic often emerges where children are assigned distinct roles: the "golden child" and the "scapegoat." These roles not only profoundly influence children's behavior and emotional development but can also have lasting effects on their self-esteem and future relationships.

The "golden child" is idealized by the narcissistic parent and seen as a perfect extension of themselves. This child can do little or no wrong in the parent's eyes, receiving constant praise and adulation. The golden child often receives special attention and privileges compared to their siblings. This special treatment can lead the child to develop an inflated sense of self-importance and a constant need for admiration.

On the other hand, the "scapegoat" is the target of the narcissistic parent's criticisms and blame. This child is continually belittled and blamed for everything that goes wrong in the family. The scapegoat receives little positive attention and is often treated with disdain and hostility. This negative treatment can deeply undermine the child's self-esteem and lead to feelings of inferiority and insecurity.

These rigidly assigned roles create significant tension within the family. The golden child, perceiving their privileged status, may develop arrogant attitudes and a sense of superiority towards their siblings and peers. Conversely, the scapegoat may feel isolated and unloved, struggling to gain the approval that seems reserved solely for the golden child.

This family dynamic is not only harmful to the scapegoat but also to the golden child. Although the golden child may seem advantaged, the excessive idealization by the narcissistic parent can prevent them from developing a realistic sense of self and their abilities. The constant need to maintain the perfect image imposed by the parent can be exhausting and create unsustainable pressure.

For the scapegoat, the constant disdain and lack of support can have devastating effects. This child may grow up with a deep sense of inadequacy and struggle to build healthy, trusting relationships. Often, scapegoats develop coping behaviors, such as submission or rebellion, in an attempt to deal with the hostility and emotional abuse.

It's important to note that these roles are not fixed and can change over time. The narcissistic parent may shift their attention and alter the roles based on circumstances and their emotional needs. However, regardless of these changes, the underlying dynamic remains dysfunctional and harmful to all family members.

Understand the Trauma Bond Forged by Narcissistic Parents

Trauma bonding is a complex phenomenon that occurs in abusive relationships, where the victim develops a deep and dysfunctional attachment to the abuser. This type of bond is particularly dangerous because it creates an emotional dependency that makes it difficult for the victim to recognize the abuse and leave. Understanding how trauma bonding develops and how to break this cycle is essential for protecting children and promoting their healing.

Trauma bonding can profoundly affect not only the victimized parent but also the children. They may be exposed to cycles of abuse and intermittent affection, creating confusion and emotional instability. The narcissist alternates between emotional abuse, severe criticism, and manipulation with moments of affection, remorse, and reconciliation. This creates emotional confusion in the victim, who begins to hope that the affection is genuine and that the abuse is just a temporary exception.

One of the key aspects of trauma bonding is the infantilization of the victim and the children. Through control and manipulation, the abuser reduces family members to a state of emotional dependency similar to that of a child towards a parent. This process is extremely destabilizing because the children gradually lose the ability to trust their own judgment and emotions. They start to see the narcissistic parent as an omnipotent figure, whose love and approval are essential for their emotional survival.

Manipulation plays a crucial role in the development of trauma bonding. The narcissist uses manipulation techniques such as gaslighting, where the victim is made to doubt their perception of reality, and love bombing, where they are intermittently flooded with affection and attention. These techniques create a psychological environment where the children become increasingly dependent on the abuser for validation and emotional security.

To protect the children, it is essential to recognize these behavior patterns and take steps to break the trauma bond cycle. The non-narcissistic parent must create a safe and stable environment where the children can freely express their feelings without fear of retaliation. Actively listening to their feelings, acknowledging their emotions, and providing age-appropriate explanations can help the children understand the situation without feeling compelled to choose between parents.

How to Stop the Narcissist from Gaslighting Your Child

Gaslighting is a subtle form of psychological manipulation where one person tries to make another doubt their own perception of reality, memories, or judgment. This phenomenon can be particularly harmful when the victims are children, as their trust in adults and their ability to understand the world are still developing. In the context of co-parenting with a narcissist, gaslighting can become a serious and widespread issue, as the narcissistic parent uses this tactic to maintain control and power.

Family dynamics can further complicate the situation. In many cases, children are gaslighted by a narcissistic parent, but the problem can also extend to other family members or significant adults in the child's life, such as uncles, grandparents, or family friends. These adults might not realize what is happening or, worse, might unknowingly contribute to the psychological manipulation to maintain a façade of family harmony.

A crucial aspect to consider is that if an adult was gaslighted as a child, seeing the same treatment inflicted on another child can be particularly painful. This is especially true if the child is someone they care deeply about, such as their own child, a niece or nephew, or a friend's child. The sensitivity to these dynamics comes from personal knowledge of the pain and confusion caused by gaslighting.

Unfortunately, authoritarian structures and family systems often fail to protect gaslighted children. Institutions that are supposed to ensure the safety and well-being of children, such as schools and social services, may not be equipped to recognize and address gaslighting. These structures tend to promote conformity and obedience, which can exacerbate the problem. Children are often instructed to accept what adults say without question, making it even harder for them to recognize and resist gaslighting.

Family dynamics can protect manipulative adults rather than children. Families often seek to maintain a certain image and may deny or minimize abusive behavior to avoid conflict or scandal. This leaves children without adequate support, trapped in a distorted reality that undermines their confidence and security. Moreover, children have an innate need for attachment and security from their parents or caregivers. This fundamental need leads them to trust the adults around them, even when those adults do not have their best interests at heart. As a result, gaslighted children tend to develop mechanisms to justify the abusive behavior, such as "Mommy is just angry" or "Daddy is just tired."

Gaslighting can manifest in various ways within the family. A parent might deny events that happened, invalidate the child's feelings, or contradict objective facts about school or peers. For example, a parent might say, "I never hit you," when they did, or might instruct the child not to reveal what happens at home to other adults, creating a forced collusion to keep painful secrets. This type of manipulation not only confuses the child but also forces them to live in a parallel reality where their experiences and feelings are constantly denied and invalidated.

In other situations, an external adult might try to call out the gaslighter's behavior, only to be contradicted and delegitimized in front of the child. For instance, if a relative or friend tells the gaslighter, "I saw you yelling at the child, that's not okay," the gaslighter might respond, "I wasn't yelling, mind your own business." This not only reinforces the gaslighting but can also further isolate the child from potential external support.

The family context of co-parenting with a narcissist makes gaslighting a particularly complex and ingrained problem. Children raised in such environments quickly learn to doubt themselves and justify their parents' abusive behavior. These toxic dynamics can have profound and lasting effects on a child's emotional and psychological development, undermining their ability to trust others and themselves for a lifetime.

Psychological Effects of Gaslighting on Children

Gaslighting can have a devastating impact on the emotional and psychological development of children. When a child is constantly exposed to this type of manipulation, their ability to trust their own perceptions and feelings is deeply undermined. This manipulation not only creates confusion and insecurity but also leads to a series of long-term consequences that can persist into adulthood.

One of the most immediate effects of gaslighting is confusion. Children, who expect to rely on adults to understand the world around them, begin to doubt their ability to correctly interpret reality when adults systematically deny their experiences or emotions. This continuous questioning of their perceptions leads to a sense of insecurity that can extend to many aspects of the child's life, causing a profound fracture in their trust in themselves and others.

The insecurity generated by gaslighting often leads children to develop defense mechanisms to cope with the situation. They may attempt to rationalize the actions of the parent or caregiver, thinking that they are just stressed or having a bad day. While this allows them to maintain some degree of emotional security in the short term, it prevents them from recognizing and addressing the abusive nature of the behavior they are subjected to.

In the long term, gaslighting can lead to profound and lasting consequences. Children exposed to this manipulation can develop significant psychological problems, such as anxiety and depression. The sense of isolation, stemming from the perception that they cannot share their true emotions and thoughts with others, can manifest in anxious and depressive behaviors, as well as difficulties in interpersonal relationships. For example, a child who has been gaslighted might struggle to trust classmates or teachers, showing withdrawal or aggressive behavior.

In a school setting, gaslighted children may encounter behavioral problems such as difficulty concentrating and disciplinary issues. The inability to process emotional trauma can result in inconsistent academic performance and difficulty forming positive relationships with peers. This is often exacerbated by the lack of understanding and support from educational institutions, which may not be equipped to recognize and address the signs of gaslighting.

Gaslighting not only undermines the child's trust in themselves but can also affect their future relationships. Children accustomed to doubting their own perceptions and justifying abusive behavior tend to replicate these dynamics in future relationships, both friendships and romantic ones. This cycle of abuse can perpetuate through generations, with victims of gaslighting often unconsciously repeating the same patterns with their own children.

The dynamics of gaslighting can be further complicated when they involve siblings. One sibling may manipulate the situation to blame another, especially if the parents tend to favor one child. These dynamics often occur in families with scapegoat and golden child roles, increasing the confusion and sense of injustice for the victimized sibling.

The emotional trauma suffered by gaslighted children can lead them to develop dysfunctional attachment bonds, known as trauma bonds. In these cases, the child continues to seek the approval and affection of the abusive parent, despite the harmful behavior. This dysfunctional bond can make it even more difficult for the child to recognize and escape abusive dynamics.

In conclusion, the psychological effects of gaslighting on children are pervasive and long-lasting. The constant manipulation of their perceptions and feelings not only undermines their self-esteem but also sets the stage for future relational and psychological problems. It is essential to recognize and intervene in these dynamics to break the cycle of abuse and provide children with a safe and healthy environment in which to grow.

How to Help Your Child Dealing With Gaslighting

Recognizing gaslighting in children is the first step in protecting your child from a narcissistic parent. Gaslighting can manifest in various ways, both direct and indirect, and understanding these forms is essential for effective intervention.

Direct gaslighting occurs when an adult openly denies events that the child knows happened, invalidates the child's feelings, or contradicts objective facts. For example, a parent might say, "I never hit you," when they actually did, or claim that the child is exaggerating their emotions by saying, "You have no reason to be sad." Another example of direct gaslighting is when a parent convinces the child to lie about what happens at home, perhaps saying, "Don't tell the doctor I punished you," or "Don't tell anyone what happened."

Indirect gaslighting, on the other hand, happens when another adult intervenes and is delegitimized by the gaslighter in front of the child. For instance, a relative might tell the gaslighter, "I saw you yelling at the child, that's not okay," and the gaslighter might respond, "I wasn't yelling, mind your own business." This not only reinforces the manipulation but can also further isolate the child from potential external support, making the gaslighter even harder to counter.

To effectively respond to gaslighting, it's crucial to listen to and validate the child's feelings. When a child feels gaslighted, their reality is constantly being questioned, which can deeply undermine their self-esteem and trust in themselves. An attentive parent can make a significant difference simply by acknowledging and accepting the child's emotions. If a child says, "Mom told me I shouldn't feel sad," the parent can respond with, "It's okay to feel sad sometimes, tell me what's making you feel this way." This simple act of listening and validation can help the child feel seen and understood, countering the destabilizing effect of gaslighting.

Another effective strategy is to create a safe space for the child, where they can freely express their emotions without fear of judgment or invalidation. This can be done through activities such as play, art, music, or other forms of creative expression. These activities allow the child to explore and communicate their feelings in a natural and safe way. For example, a parent might encourage the child to draw what they are feeling or tell a story that reflects their emotions. These moments of free expression can be therapeutic and help the child process their experiences.

It is also crucial that the parent never gaslights their own child. Even unintentionally, invalidating the child's feelings can have similar negative effects to those of gaslighting perpetrated by the narcissistic parent. Phrases like "You shouldn't feel that way" or "You're overreacting" may seem harmless but can contribute to undermining the child's trust in their own emotions. Instead, phrases like "I understand that you feel this way, it's normal" or "You can always talk to me about how you feel" can make a big difference in building an environment of trust and emotional safety.

It's important to regularly monitor the child's emotional state. Asking how they feel, talking about their day, and being available to listen can help identify any signs of distress or manipulation. An attentive and present parent can often notice changes in the child's behavior or mood that might indicate the presence of gaslighting.

Chapter 14:
Why Narcissists Don't Truly Love Their Kids

They Show Affection Only in Public to Gain Approval

Narcissistic parents show affection towards their children primarily in public, with the sole aim of gaining admiration and approval from others. This public display of affection is nothing more than a performance to build and maintain a positive self-image in the eyes of society. However, in private, their behavior changes drastically. The narcissistic parent can become detached, uninterested, and even cruel.

This duality is evident in their contradictory behaviors: in the presence of others, the narcissistic parent may be affectionate and attentive, acting like the ideal parent. Yet, once back in the privacy of their home, the affection disappears, leaving the child confused and hurt. This unstable and unpredictable behavior creates a traumatic and disorienting dynamic for the child, who struggles to understand the reason behind these changes.

The true goal of the narcissistic parent is never the child's well-being, but rather the enhancement of their own public image. Such a parent is not interested in the child's happiness or development, but only in how the public display of attention and affection can reflect positively on them.

They Idealize the Toddler Stage for Personal Gratification

Narcissists tend to idealize the toddler stage of their children's lives because, during this period, they receive abundant attention and compliments from others about their children. In early childhood, children do not yet speak and are completely dependent on their parents for all their needs. This total dependence is seen by narcissists as the highest form of gratification because the children are obedient and easy to control.

During this stage, the narcissist is not interested in the child's development but rather in the role they themselves play in the eyes of others. They receive approval and admiration simply for being parents, without having to deal with the complexities of the child's growth and individuality. This type of affection is shallow and serves only to satisfy the narcissistic parent's need for validation.

As children grow and start to develop their own personalities, narcissists reveal their true nature. The individuation phase, where the child begins to express their uniqueness, becomes problematic. The narcissist cannot tolerate independence and autonomy because they see the child as personal property to control and shape in their own image. The transition from the toddler stage to adolescence often marks the beginning of a colder and more distant treatment, as the child no longer fulfills the narcissist's need for approval and control.

They Use Control and Conformity as a Form of Domination

Narcissists use control and conformity as their main tools to dominate their children. During childhood and adolescence, especially between the ages of 3 and 15, children are less likely to question authority. This period is particularly advantageous for narcissistic parents, who find it easier to shape their children according to their own image and desires.

Narcissists choose what their children should study, who their friends should be, and how they should behave. Every aspect of the child's life is decided by the parent, depriving the child of the opportunity to develop their own identity. This constant imposition of control is often mistaken for affection or interest, but in reality, it is a form of manipulation to maintain power.

When the child begins to express their individuality or develop traits that set them apart from the parent, the narcissist sees this as a threat. Any attempt at independence is perceived as an act of rebellion and is met with hostility. The narcissist attacks and tries to suppress the child's emerging identity, punishing any differences in opinion or behavior that do not exactly reflect their own expectations.

This cycle of control and repression creates an environment where the child grows up with the constant feeling of needing to earn the parent's love and approval, living in a perpetual state of anxiety and insecurity.

They Offer Conditional Love

Narcissists offer love and attention to their children only conditionally, basing their affection on the child's performance and achievements. Unlike healthy parents, who show unconditional acceptance towards their children, narcissists use love as a bargaining tool, giving it only when the child meets their expectations and desires.

This conditionality manifests in the way narcissistic parents reward or punish their children. Affection and attention are given only when the child does things that reflect positively on the parent, such as getting good grades, excelling in extracurricular activities, or behaving in a way that makes others praise the parent for their "good parenting." In the absence of such performances, the child is devalued and ignored, experiencing a drastic withdrawal of attention and love.

As a result of this behavior, children of narcissists grow up with a distorted perception of love and self-worth. They learn that love is something to be earned, not an inherent right, and that their value depends on their ability to please the parent. This dynamic can lead to severe self-esteem issues and a persistent need for external validation, as the child, now an adult, continues to seek the recognition they never genuinely received during their childhood.

They Use Children as Tools of Manipulation

Narcissists often use their children as tools of manipulation to achieve their own goals. Instead of seeing their children as individuals with their own needs and desires, they treat them as pawns to influence and control situations or people around them. Children are dragged into adult issues, forced to act as mediators, therapists, or to bear burdens they cannot understand or resolve.

A common example is using children to punish the other parent during conflicts. Narcissists may manipulate their children to take sides against the other parent, creating alliances that increase their power and control within the family. In cases of divorce or separation, children become tools to gain legal or emotional advantages, leaving them confused and traumatized.

Unaware they are being manipulated, children often do not realize they are being used until the damage is already done. They grow up in an environment where their worth is tied to their utility to the narcissistic parent, rather than being valued as individuals with their own identities. This can have devastating effects on their emotional and psychological development, leaving them with a sense of emptiness and worthlessness.

The ongoing manipulation creates a cycle of emotional dependence, where children constantly strive to please the parent to avoid punishment or to receive rare displays of affection. This toxic dynamic undermines their ability to form healthy and autonomous relationships in the future.

They Create the Facade of a Perfect Family

Narcissists have a deep-seated need to project the image of a perfect family. This obsession with appearance leads them to focus on their children's outward looks, manners, and achievements, using them as a reflection of their parenting skills. The image of the ideal family becomes more important than the actual substance of family relationships, resulting in a lack of genuine emotional depth.

Children are often forced to maintain unrealistic standards to meet the narcissistic parent's expectations. They must always look well-groomed, behave impeccably, and achieve outstanding results in every area, all to feed the illusion of a perfect family. This creates immense pressure on the children, who constantly feel scrutinized and fear disappointing the parent.

The exclusive focus on outward appearances also leads to the creation of rigid roles within the family, such as the "golden child" and the "scapegoat." The golden child is the one who perfectly mirrors the parent's expectations and thus receives praise and privileges. In contrast, the scapegoat is the child who fails to conform and is therefore constantly devalued and criticized.

This dynamic of favoritism and devaluation not only undermines the children's self-esteem but also creates divisions and conflicts among siblings. The result is a family that appears perfect on the outside but is internally fragmented and devoid of true emotional connections. Children grow up learning that their family's value is based solely on the image they can project, rather than the quality of their relationships.

They Favor and Divide to Maintain Control

Narcissists favor one child over the others to create divisions and maintain control within the family. This favoritism is not based on genuine affection but is a deliberate strategy to manipulate and dominate. By favoring one child, the narcissist creates alliances that strengthen their power and isolate the other children, leading to a toxic and competitive family dynamic.

The favored child, often referred to as the "golden child," receives praise, privileges, and special attention, while the other children, such as the "scapegoat," are constantly devalued and criticized. This disparity in treatment creates tensions and rivalries among siblings, who struggle to gain the narcissistic parent's approval. The favored child becomes an ally of the parent, often unaware of the manipulative role they are playing.

This manipulation further divides the family, making it difficult for the children to form strong and supportive bonds with each other. The constant need to compete for the parent's attention and approval creates an environment of insecurity and distrust. The children grow up learning that affection and self-worth are contingent on their ability to meet the narcissist's demands and expectations.

The result of this dynamic is a fragmented family, where relationships are based on competition and manipulation rather than love and mutual support. As adults, the children may struggle to establish healthy relationships and trust others, carrying the emotional scars of a childhood dominated by favoritism and division.

They Use Their Children to Avoid Their Own Emotional Void

Narcissists often use their children to fill the emotional void they feel within themselves. Unable to confront their own insecurities and deficiencies, they project their emotional needs onto their children. Unwittingly, the children become the means through which the narcissistic parent seeks to satisfy their need for affection, attention, and validation that they cannot obtain elsewhere.

This behavior forces the children into an inappropriate role, becoming the caretakers of the parent's emotions. The children are required to be constantly present and available to offer emotional support, reassurance, and admiration. The narcissistic parent depends on the child to feel worthy and important, completely ignoring the child's emotional needs.

The resulting relationship is profoundly unbalanced. The child does not receive the necessary support and affection for healthy emotional development, as they are continually engaged in meeting the parent's needs. This creates a cycle of emotional dependency, where the child feels obligated to fulfill the parent's needs to obtain a semblance of love and approval.

In the long term, children of narcissists who grow up in such dynamics often develop self-esteem issues and difficulties in interpersonal relationships. They have been conditioned to set aside their own feelings and needs to prioritize those of the parent, and they may struggle to establish healthy boundaries and recognize their own worth as independent individuals.

Chapter 15:
Building a Healthy Relationship After Abuse

The healing process after a narcissistic relationship is complex and often marked by a profound change in how one perceives relationships. One crucial aspect of this healing is the ability to discern, which means making thoughtful and informed choices about the people with whom we establish new relationships. Discernment should not be confused with being picky. While the former involves a careful and respectful evaluation of oneself and others, the latter often results in superficial judgments based on irrelevant criteria.

After experiencing a narcissistic relationship, many people feel they can no longer endure the mental manipulations and reality distortions they have faced. This leads to a deep mistrust of future relationships, a feeling of being trapped in a loop of suspicion and fear of being hurt again. For some, this experience creates a deep-seated belief that they will never be able to enter a healthy relationship again. The loss of trust and security becomes an insurmountable barrier, with many finding themselves having to balance the desire for intimacy with the terror of repeating the same mistakes.

On the other end of the spectrum, there are those who, out of fear of being alone, quickly dive into new relationships without giving themselves the necessary time to heal. This behavior can be just as dangerous, leading to a cycle of unhealthy relationships, each potentially inflicting new emotional wounds.

The key to overcoming these obstacles lies in learning the difference between blind trust and informed discernment. Many survivors of narcissistic relationships see themselves as "damaged" or "broken" because they find it difficult to trust others. They feel guilty for keeping their defenses up and often face external pressure to lower them. Comments like "Not everyone is like your narcissistic ex" or "If you keep looking for red flags, you'll find them" are common but can be harmful, prompting individuals to ignore warning signs just to avoid being judged.

Our culture tends to glorify fast and intense love stories, fueling the idea that an immediate connection equates to true love. This myth of "love at first sight" and "soulmates" can make those who prefer a more measured and reflective approach to relationships seem pathological. Often, cautious individuals are viewed as too distrustful or unable to let go, while those who jump in headfirst are seen as brave and authentic.

In reality, prudence and taking things slowly in building a relationship are signs of maturity and self-esteem. Recognizing and accepting that your pace may be slower than others is a fundamental step toward healing. The ability to discern is not a weakness but a strength that allows you to protect yourself and avoid falling back into toxic dynamics.

Being discerning means giving yourself the necessary time to evaluate whether a new person deserves your trust. It is an act of self-respect that involves recognizing your worth and refusing to settle for less just to avoid loneliness. This form of discernment is particularly important for those who have survived abusive relationships, as it protects them from further emotional harm and promotes authentic and lasting healing.

Discernment also involves accepting that trust must be earned. It's not about being cold or distant but about establishing healthy boundaries and not succumbing to external pressures to grant unearned trust. This respectful approach towards oneself is a key element in avoiding new disappointments and building future relationships on solid and healthy foundations.

Understanding the importance of discernment is just the beginning. To better comprehend how our romantic culture influences our view of relationships and how to develop this valuable skill, we need to explore the impact of "magical and rapid romance" and how discernment can truly transform our approach to relationships.

Rapid Romantic Culture and Discernment

Our romantic culture is steeped in myths about "love at first sight" and "soulmates," promoting the idea that true relationships must develop quickly and intensely. This "magical and rapid romance" model often makes those who take a more measured and reflective approach to relationships seem pathological. However, this romantic narrative can be dangerous, especially for those who have already experienced narcissistic abuse.

The impulsiveness in seeking a soulmate and moving quickly in a relationship can lead to ignoring obvious red flags. Many narcissistic relationships start this way, with a rapid escalation of emotions that masks problematic behaviors. The allure of an immediate connection can cause people to overlook fundamental aspects such as long-term compatibility, mutual respect, and emotional stability.

Being discerning, on the other hand, involves a deliberate and careful approach. It means taking the necessary time to truly get to know a new person, evaluate their behaviors, and see if their values and actions align with your expectations of respect, kindness, and reciprocity. This is not any less romantic; in fact, building a relationship based on deep knowledge and mutual respect creates a solid and enduring foundation.

Discernment as part of healing also requires recognizing your own worth. Many survivors of narcissistic abuse were never encouraged to value themselves. Even before meeting their narcissist, they often didn't learn to see their trust as a precious gift that must be earned. Instead, they were often led to believe they should accept any attention just to avoid being alone, thus perpetuating cycles of toxic relationships.

Rediscovering and developing discernment also means being at peace with your own solitude and appreciating your own company. It means not defining yourself through the presence of a relationship but through the quality of the relationships you choose to have. The fear of loneliness should never be a reason to accept less than you deserve.

Being discerning does not mean being elitist or unreasonably demanding, such as rejecting someone for superficial reasons like appearance or material possessions. Instead, it means paying attention to deep and substantial characteristics like kindness, compassion, reciprocity, respect, self-awareness, and the ability to see and support the other as a whole person.

Discernment is a kind of superpower in healing from narcissistic relationships. It allows you to protect yourself from further harm and build healthier, more satisfying relationships. However, society often tends to label discernment as coldness, distance, or fussiness. Words matter, and shifting your language from "trust issues" to "discernment" can help remove the filters that obscure the view of warning signs and allow you to take your time in new relationships.

Many people, unfortunately, do not believe they deserve better and are paralyzed by the fear of being alone. This leads to a "settle for what you can get" mentality, preventing them from taking the necessary time to be discerning. But being discerning in critical decisions, such as choosing a person to spend your life with or a colleague to work with long-term, is crucial.

Discernment is a key element in the healing process from narcissistic relationships. It is a skill that allows you to build healthier and more fulfilling relationships based on respect, reciprocity, and authenticity. Learning to be discerning means recognizing your own worth, respecting yourself, and having the courage to wait for what is truly deserving of your trust.

Dealing with Emotional Dysregulation First

One of the first challenges to face after experiencing an abusive relationship is emotional dysregulation. When we come out of a relationship with a manipulative or narcissistic partner, we often find ourselves in a state of great emotional confusion. This state, known as emotional dysregulation, distorts our perceptions and prevents us from seeing things as they truly are.

Emotional abusers attack our confidence and our sense of reality, creating a condition where our emotions are out of control. This leads to distorted perceptions, making it difficult for us to recognize the truth and make informed decisions. Therefore, it's crucial to work on re-establishing emotional balance before even considering entering a new relationship.

One of the first questions many people ask is: how can I start to regulate my emotions? The answer often begins with understanding emotional flashbacks. Emotional flashbacks are intrusive and intense memories that bring past traumatic experiences to the forefront, causing strong and seemingly unjustified emotional reactions. These flashbacks can be triggered by situations that vaguely remind us of the abuse we endured.

To manage these flashbacks, it's helpful to learn how to recognize them and reduce their intensity. A practical method is to focus on the present, using grounding techniques. These techniques can include awareness of your breath, detailed descriptions of your surroundings, or concentrating on specific physical sensations, like the contact of your feet with the ground. These exercises help bring the mind back to the present moment, reducing the impact of the flashbacks.

It's also crucial to develop emotional literacy, the ability to identify, understand, and manage your emotions. This process includes self-reflection and analyzing your emotional states, recognizing the triggers that provoke intense reactions, and developing strategies to deal with them. For example, keeping an emotion journal can be an excellent practice to increase self-awareness and track progress over time.

In addition to managing flashbacks and developing emotional literacy, it's important to consider the time needed to heal. There is no set time frame for recovery after an abusive relationship, but it's essential to take the necessary time to address and resolve emotional pain. Only then can you be truly ready for a new, healthy, and fulfilling relationship.

Where Does CPTSD Come From?

To fully understand the complex trauma that can emerge from an abusive relationship, it's essential to explore the roots of Complex Post-Traumatic Stress Disorder (CPTSD). This disorder doesn't arise solely from isolated traumatic events but is the result of prolonged exposure to situations of abuse and emotional manipulation.

Abusive relationships often begin with small acts of manipulation that, over time, become increasingly intense and frequent. These acts aim to undermine our self-esteem and destabilize our sense of reality. However, CPTSD isn't exclusively the result of a single abusive relationship. Many people who develop CPTSD have a history of childhood trauma. Growing up in a dysfunctional family environment, where emotional needs are not met or where one is subjected to emotional, physical, or psychological abuse, lays the groundwork for future toxic relationships.

Childhood traumas can manifest in various ways. For example, if our primary caregivers were excessively demanding, intrusive, or manipulative, we might develop a form of chronic stress that affects our emotional development. If left unaddressed, this stress can lead to dysfunctional behaviors and increased vulnerability to abusive relationships in adulthood. It's as if our brains are programmed to seek out familiar patterns, even if they are harmful.

CPTSD doesn't only stem from childhood traumas. Traumatic experiences in adulthood, such as a relationship with a narcissistic partner or someone with cluster B personality disorders (like borderline or antisocial disorders), can also lead to the development of CPTSD. These relationships are characterized by constant emotional and psychological bombardment, making us feel trapped and helpless.

One of the most challenging aspects of CPTSD is the presence of emotional flashbacks. These flashbacks differ from typical PTSD flashbacks, which are often visual. Emotional flashbacks are sudden and overwhelming emotional episodes that seem to come out of nowhere, taking us back to the original trauma. They can be triggered by everyday situations that vaguely remind us of the abuse we endured.

Another critical component of CPTSD is the sense of hyper-vigilance and altered perception of reality. People with CPTSD often live in a state of constant alertness, always ready to defend themselves against potential threats. This continuous state of tension makes it difficult to relax and trust others, hindering the formation of healthy relationships.

It's important to emphasize that CPTSD is a natural response to extremely adverse and prolonged situations, not a weakness or personal flaw. Understanding this distinction is crucial for beginning the healing process. Recognizing and accepting one's traumatic past is the first step toward freeing oneself from its effects and building a healthier, more serene life.

An effective approach to dealing with CPTSD is to work with a therapist specialized in complex trauma. Therapy can help identify and understand the defense mechanisms developed over the years and replace them with healthier, more functional coping strategies. Additionally, participating in support groups with people who have experienced similar situations can provide a sense of community and understanding, which is often crucial in the healing process.

Hijacking The Super-Ego

To understand how trauma deeply affects our psyche, we need to explore the concept of the super-ego and how it can be hijacked by traumatic experiences. The super-ego is that part of our mind that stands above the ego, serving as a moral guide. It tells us what is right and wrong based on the values and norms internalized during our upbringing.

In a healthy environment, the super-ego helps us live in harmony with our values and social expectations. However, in the presence of traumatic experiences, such as emotional abuse or psychological manipulation, the super-ego can be hijacked, becoming an extremely negative inner critic. This happens because the super-ego absorbs and reproduces the harmful messages received during the abuse.

When the super-ego is hijacked, it turns into a kind of mental "software virus." Instead of protecting and guiding us, the hijacked super-ego sends damaging messages, making us believe we are unworthy of love and respect. This inner critic might tell us that we are inherently flawed, that we don't deserve happiness, and that every mistake we make is proof of our inadequacy.

These negative messages not only erode our self-esteem but also constantly make us relive past pain, reinforcing a cycle of self-sabotage.

The hijacking of the super-ego often occurs in dysfunctional family environments or abusive relationships. When our primary caregivers are manipulative or abusive, the super-ego absorbs these behaviors and reproduces them internally. This leads to an inner critic that does not reflect reality but incessantly repeats the negative messages received in the past.

To free ourselves from the influence of a hijacked super-ego, it is necessary to recognize and challenge these internal messages. This requires deep work of awareness and cognitive restructuring. It is important to identify these negative messages as remnants of our traumatic experiences and not as absolute truths.

A crucial step is developing self-compassion. Self-compassion helps us treat ourselves with the same kindness and understanding that we would offer a dear friend. This means acknowledging our pain, accepting it without judgment, and offering ourselves words of comfort and encouragement.

5 CPTSD Behaviors That Damage Relationships

This section will explore five typical CPTSD behaviors that, if left unaddressed, can damage relationships. Understanding these behaviors is the first step toward overcoming them and beginning to build healthier and more fulfilling relationships. With the right awareness and adequate support, it is possible to break toxic cycles and open up to new opportunities for authentic connection.

1. Overexposure and Underdevelopment in Relationships

Have you ever noticed how sometimes we tend to share too much about ourselves too soon? Imagine meeting someone for the first time and, within a few minutes, sharing the most intimate details of your life. This behavior can be rooted in our trauma response, especially if our main response has been to appease.

During a long period of a toxic relationship, like the one with a malignant narcissist, we were forced to sacrifice our true selves to avoid conflicts and punishments. This developed in us the habit of seeking others' approval at any cost. So, when we meet someone new, our instinct is to overshare in the hope of being accepted and appreciated. However, this can be overwhelming for those who are not used to such intense relationships from the start.

On the other hand, some of us might do the exact opposite: share too little. If our trauma response was to "freeze," we might appear detached or lacking in personality. This happens because we were punished in the past for showing our true selves, and now we prefer not to reveal ourselves at all to avoid pain. Both of these dynamics can sabotage our attempts to build healthy relationships, creating barriers that further isolate us.

2. Lack of Trust and Hypervigilance Toward Narcissistic Traits

After experiencing abuse from a narcissist, our brain can become extremely sensitive to any signal that might indicate narcissistic behavior in others. This is linked to the reticular activating system, a part of our brain that acts as a filter, helping us notice what we consider important.

Imagine spending years watching videos and reading articles about narcissistic abuse, with strong emotions tied to these experiences. Your brain starts to consider narcissistic traits as highly relevant and, as a result, begins to notice them everywhere. This can lead to a state of hypervigilance, where we see narcissists around every corner, even when they aren't there. For example, a simple smile might be interpreted as a narcissistic smirk, or an innocent comment might seem like an attempt at gaslighting.

This hypervigilance can severely compromise our ability to trust others. We live in a constant state of alert, always ready to identify and reject any sign of abuse. This state of constant suspicion makes it difficult to form genuine bonds because we're too busy scrutinizing every detail to be truly present with people. Trust, which is fundamental for any healthy relationship, becomes almost impossible to develop.

To overcome this barrier, it's essential to re-educate our reticular activating system, helping our brain distinguish between real danger signals and false alarms. This takes time and practice, but with awareness and the right help, we can learn to relax and give others the benefit of the doubt, allowing us to build relationships based on trust and mutual respect.

3. Emotional Triggers and Disproportionate Reactions

Have you ever overreacted to a seemingly harmless situation, wondering why your response was so intense? This is a common phenomenon for those suffering from CPTSD. Emotional triggers can cause disproportionate reactions, often linked to unresolved wounds from the past.

Imagine being at work and a colleague makes a comment that seems critical. Suddenly, you feel a wave of anger or sadness that seems excessive for the situation. This happens because the comment touched a deep wound, reactivating emotions tied to past experiences of abuse or neglect. When we are triggered, we are not responding to the present situation, but reacting to an entire history of pain and trauma.

These reactions can strain our relationships, as others may not understand the intensity of our responses. A friend who makes an innocent remark might be met with our defensive or aggressive reaction, without understanding why. This can create misunderstandings and distance, making it difficult to maintain healthy and stable relationships.

4. Difficulty Letting Go of the Past

Have you ever felt trapped in an endless cycle of thoughts about the past? This is a common issue for those who have experienced significant trauma and suffer from CPTSD. The mind tends to repeatedly revisit painful experiences, making it hard to live in the present.

After leaving a toxic relationship, many find their minds constantly replaying the same traumatic experiences. These repetitive thoughts can become so pervasive that they feel like part of our identity. It's as if the pain of the past becomes a label we carry, influencing every aspect of our current life.

This attachment to the past can seriously hinder our ability to build healthy relationships. When our mind is constantly focused on the past, it's challenging to be fully present with others. We might miss important moments and fail to truly connect with those around us. Additionally, this focus on past traumas can lead us to misinterpret the actions and intentions of people in the present, seeing threats where there are none.

5. Passive-Aggressive Behaviors

Imagine being in a situation where you feel that expressing your feelings will only lead to conflict and punishment. This scenario may seem familiar to those who have suffered narcissistic abuse, often leading to the development of passive-aggressive behaviors. When we have been punished for showing our true emotions, we learn to hide them, but repressed emotions still find a way to emerge.

These passive-aggressive behaviors can manifest in subtle but damaging ways, such as silent treatment, sarcastic comments, or intentional procrastination. For instance, you might avoid addressing an issue with your partner and instead choose to ignore it, hoping they will understand your discontent on their own. This kind of indirect communication only creates tension and misunderstandings, further damaging the relationship.

The main problem with passive-aggressive behaviors is that they do not resolve conflicts but exacerbate them. Repressed emotions do not disappear; they accumulate and eventually explode at inopportune moments, often leading to overreactions that can frighten and push away those close to us. It is a vicious cycle that can make it difficult to establish healthy and genuine relationships.

To break this cycle, it is essential to learn to communicate more openly and directly. Practicing assertiveness can be a valuable aid: expressing your feelings and needs clearly and respectfully is fundamental to building and maintaining healthy relationships.

Your Feedback Matters

Dear reader,

I thank you from the bottom of my heart for making it this far. I hope you have found the reading of my book useful. Facing the challenges of co-parenting with a narcissist can be incredibly demanding, and I appreciate you taking the time to explore the strategies and advice shared here.

Your journey is unique, but by sharing your honest opinion of this book on Amazon, you can help others who are facing similar struggles. Your review can guide other parents to valuable information and support, showing them that they are not alone in this journey.

As an author, feedback can have a significant impact on the success of my book. I would be very grateful if you could write a review on Amazon in your free time. I will read it personally and appreciate all feedback, both positive and negative.

Click here to leave your review on Amazon.

Your comments are invaluable, and I thank you for your time and support.

Sincerely,
Melanie Wolfkill

A Final note

As we reach the end of this journey together, I want to congratulate you on the resilience and strength you have shown in embarking on this path of personal growth. I hope my book has provided you with the tools to face this complex challenge with confidence and renewed hope.

You have learned the importance of setting firm boundaries and maintaining clear communication to protect yourself and your children. You have discovered the value of staying calm and composed in the face of manipulation and conflict, ensuring that your children's well-being remains the top priority. Most importantly, you have understood how crucial your mental and emotional health is.

Now it is time to put these lessons into practice. Take the knowledge you have gained and apply it to your daily life. Establish routines that reinforce stability for your children, and do not hesitate to seek help when you need it. Remember, every step you take towards a healthier co-parenting dynamic is a step towards a brighter future for you and your family.

Start by implementing a new strategy from this book today. Whether it's setting a new boundary, having a conversation with your support network, or taking a moment for self-care, small steps can lead to significant changes. Continue to educate yourself and seek out resources that can further support you on this journey.

I want to thank you for allowing me to be part of your journey. Writing this book has been a deeply personal experience, and my hope is that it provides you with the guidance and encouragement you need. Co-parenting with a narcissist is never easy, but remember that you are not alone. There is a community of individuals who understand your struggle and are ready to support you.

Good luck on your journey. May you find peace, strength, and joy as you move forward. You have the power to create a positive and nurturing environment for your children, and I believe in your ability to do so.

With sincere wishes for your success,

Melanie

About the Author

Melanie Wolfkill is an author and consultant specializing in co-parenting with toxic ex-partners, a challenge she has personally faced. This experience has made her deeply aware of the unique difficulties it involves. Her direct knowledge has enabled her to assist numerous parents in safeguarding the emotional well-being of their children and maintaining a healthy balance during and after the separation process.

Melanie also offers couples therapy, supporting those undergoing tough separations or divorces, equipping them with effective tools to manage pain and prepare for new life stages. Her practical and compassionate approach has provided many parents with the ability to set clear boundaries and maintain their mental health in extremely stressful situations.

Melanie began writing to share her experiences and insights with a broader audience, hoping to help other parents navigate the complexities of co-parenting with a narcissistic ex. Her works offer practical advice, effective strategies, and emotional support to address the unique challenges this situation presents.

Melanie's goal is to share her experience and acquired knowledge with readers to help those in similar situations to:

- Know that they are not alone
- Identify signs of narcissistic abuse
- Take back control of their lives
- Achieve a sense of freedom and self-esteem

In her free time, Melanie enjoys spending time outdoors, practicing yoga and meditation, finding balance and inner peace. Her dedication to personal well-being and continuous growth is reflected in her work, inspiring many parents to embark on their own journey of healing and personal growth.

Printed in Great Britain
by Amazon

43921988R00106